Praise for

WHO NOT HOW

"Dan Sullivan is the ultimate coach for entrepreneurs.
I've been learning from him for over 20 years! Anyone
who reads *Who Not How* will know exactly how
the best entrepreneurs create freedom."

— **David Bach**, *New York Times* best-selling author, founder of
FinishRich.com, and co-founder of AE Wealth Management

"How do you shift your life? You shift your thinking.
And how do you shift your thinking? Dan Sullivan says
it starts by 'thinking about your thinking.' Dan is the
entrepreneur's coach of coaches because he helps you
think about your thinking to gain an entirely new
perspective that doesn't just impact your business,
it elevates every aspect of your life."

— **JJ Virgin**, CNS, CHFS, *New York Times* best-selling author
and founder of Mindshare Collaborative

"To say that I have thrived both personally and
professionally because of Dan Sullivan's coaching would
be an understatement. Dan is blessed with the innate
talent to simplify the most complex business
situations and create tools that are so easy to use.
The world is better off because of him."

— **Ninad Tipnis**, founder and principal, JTCPL Designs

"Dan Sullivan is a one-of-a-kind human being. There
is a clarity, tenacity, and conviction that just oozes
out of him. Pay close attention, and that wisdom will
rub off on you. His generosity of spirit gives you open
access to his fascinating thought process."

— **Kathy Kolbe**, brain researcher and theorist and founder
of Kolbe Corp.

"Dan is *Yoda* for entrepreneurs. His wisdom drops are perfectly timed yet timeless. His true gift is not in pouring out his wisdom but in helping entrepreneurs find their Unique Ability (aka the force) and then teaching them how to wield it, creating exponential impact and success."

— **Lisa Cini**, CEO and founder, Mosaic Design Studio and BestLivingTech.com

"I have interviewed a bucket list of the most successful, most sought-out entrepreneurs in the world. They are the ones you see on TV, the ones you know by name. I've been lucky enough to make friends with many of them and have the ability to call on them when I need advice. But there is only one person in the world who can help me not only see but achieve realities that are far bigger than I had previously imagined, and that's Dan Sullivan. My life, my business, and my relationships are 100X better because I work with Dan."

— **Nick Nanton, Esq.**, Emmy® Award-winning director and producer, *Wall Street Journal* best-selling author, and Global Shield Humanitarian Award recipient

"Dan Sullivan changes lives. He has influenced me and thousands of others who have studied with him and read his books. Pay very close attention: his rock-solid insights and wisdom will improve your life and make you money!"

— **Keith J. Cunningham**, co-founder of Keys to the Vault, best-selling author of *The Road Less Stupid*

"Dan Sullivan is a champion for entrepreneurs. He is a master at offering original solutions that amplify capabilities, leading to a path of more freedom and sustainable success. Dan Sullivan is the 'Who' I consistently turn to as my secret weapon, strengthening and guiding my capabilities successfully into the future. I am grateful he does the work!"

— **L. Lee Richter**, CEO of Richter Design Group

"Dan Sullivan is one of America's great thinkers. His understanding of the entrepreneurial mind is unrivaled. Dan has an uncanny ability to see around corners and discern what is coming next before anyone else. Dan's influence and thinking are seen and felt in many of America's most innovative and fastest-growing companies. His thinking has contributed billions of dollars to the economy. This is why those of us who know him best call him the coach's coach."

— **Mark Young, Ph.D.**, founder and CEO of Jekyll and Hyde Advertising and Marketing

"Dan Sullivan is the preeminent advisor to successful entrepreneurs worldwide. Countless of his past and present clients owe their fortunes to Dan's wisdom and coaching. I have been following Dan's teachings for nearly 20 years, and he still inspires me in so many ways."

— **John Ferrell, Esq.**, co-founder of Carr & Ferrell LLP

"Dan is the preeminent coach for successful entrepreneurs who want more from life: more freedom of purpose, time, money, and relationships. My life, and the lives of those I love, are so much richer as a direct result of applying Dan's unique wisdom and thinking tools in every area of my life."

— **Paul F. Heiss**, founder and president, IBCC Industries

"Dan Sullivan is the most creative and visionary coach for entrepreneurs working today. His insights and innovations are worth billions of dollars, and Dan's revolutionary methods unlock the secrets to your personal and professional freedom. Dan walks his talk!"

— **Steven Palter and Michele Lang Palter**, Gold Coast IVF and Lodestone Technology

WHO
NOT
HOW

ALSO BY DR. BENJAMIN HARDY

*Personality Isn't Permanent: Break Free from Self-Limiting
Beliefs and Rewrite Your Story*

Willpower Doesn't Work: Discover the Hidden Keys to Success

WHO

THE FORMULA TO ACHIEVE BIGGER GOALS

NOT

THROUGH ACCELERATING TEAMWORK

HOW

DAN SULLIVAN

FOUNDER OF **STRATEGIC COACH**

WITH **DR. BENJAMIN HARDY**

HAY HOUSE, INC.
Carlsbad, California • New York City
London • Sydney • New Delhi

Published in the United States by: Hay House, Inc.: www.hayhouse
.com® • *Published in Australia by:* Hay House Australia Pty. Ltd.: www
.hayhouse.com.au • *Published in the United Kingdom by:* Hay House UK,
Ltd.: www.hayhouse.co.uk • *Published in India by:* Hay House Publishers
India: www.hayhouse.co.in

Project editor: Melody Guy • *Indexer:* J S Editorial, LLC
Cover design: The Book Designers • *Interior design:* Nick C. Welch

Library of Congress Cataloging-in-Publication Data

Names: Sullivan, Dan, 1944- author. | Hardy, Benjamin, author.
Title: Who not how : the formula to achieve bigger goals through
   accelerating teamwork / Dan Sullivan, Founder of Strategic Coach with
   Dr. Benjamin Hardy.
Identifiers: LCCN 2020026442 | ISBN 9781401960582 (hardback) | ISBN
   9781401960599 (ebook)
Subjects: LCSH: Success. | Goal (Psychology) | Cooperation.
Classification: LCC BF637.S8 S815 2020 | DDC 658.4/022--dc23
LC record available at https://lccn.loc.gov/2020026442

Hardcover ISBN: 978-1-4019-6058-2
E-book ISBN: 978-1-4019-6059-9
Audiobook ISBN: 978-1-4019-6077-3

18 17 16 15 14 13
1st edition, October 2020

SUSTAINABLE
FORESTRY
INITIATIVE

Certified Chain of Custody
Promoting Sustainable Forestry

www.forests.org
SFI-01268

SFI label applies to the text stock

Printed in the United States of America

To **Dean Jackson**, for being the Who that gave Dan this crucial insight, and for coining the term "Who Not How."
This book would not exist without you and your brilliant mind.
Thank you for your endless inspiration and collaboration, particularly with Dan on the Joy of Procrastination Podcast.
We love you!

"Take a look at any significant innovation, and the myth of the lone genius and the 'eureka moment' breaks down."
—*Harvard Business Review*

"Edison said, 'Genius is one percent inspiration and ninety-nine percent perspiration.' But whose? His real knack was for commanding and beguiling others to execute his ideas."
—Joshua Wolf Shenk, author of *Powers of Two*

CONTENTS

INTRODUCTION

What Is Who Not How, and Why Should It Matter to You?

Michael Jordan, arguably the greatest basketball player of all time, didn't win a championship during his first six years in the NBA.

Drafted by the Chicago Bulls in 1984, Michael saw his team swept from the first round of the playoffs during his first three seasons. He was emerging as one of the best players in the league, possibly the best player, but he was lacking playoff success.

It was clear to the Bulls organization that Michael couldn't succeed at the highest level—meaning *win championships*—by himself. Although he was the most talented individual player, he needed support.

Michael Jordan needed a Who, not a How.

In 1987, the Bulls traded for the incoming rookie, Scottie Pippen, who was originally drafted by the Seattle SuperSonics. Scottie was the perfect collaborator for Michael, and he quickly adopted Michael's aggressiveness and competitive spirit. Scottie pushed Michael, sharpening his skills on both defense and offense, but he also helped him evolve from a one-man show to more of a team player.

Their first season together, the Bulls were able to get out of the first round of the playoffs. The next two seasons—1988 and 1989—the Bulls were destroyed in the second round by the more experienced and more physical Detroit Pistons. These were devastating blows. For Michael and the Bulls, though, these "failures" were exactly what they needed to deepen their commitment to their ultimate goal.

By 1989, it was no longer an argument who the best player in basketball was. Michael Jordan, as an individual talent, had no rival. And with the help of Pippen, the Bulls had broken past their former plateaus and gotten to their own next level. But even with Jordan's godly abilities, the Bulls hit another wall.

The Pistons had developed what they called the "Jordan Rules," which consisted of them double or triple teaming Jordan every time he got the ball. Once Jordan was taken out of the game, the Bulls had no chance.

The Chicago Bulls needed *another* Who, not solely more of Michael's How.

Phil Jackson became the head coach of the Chicago Bulls in 1989. Recognizing that the Bulls needed a more team-based strategy, rather than relying exclusively on Michael's superhuman talent, Jackson installed the triangle offense—a strategy for creating space on the floor with more passing and cutting to get players the open shot.

By sharing responsibility rather than shouldering it, Michael blossomed into a brilliant all-around player. His vision for what he could ultimately achieve expanded, and the Bulls realized that with an amazing team and coach, they could create something truly special and unique.

During Jackson's first year as head coach, the Bulls became a far better team, finishing the season with a 55–27 record. They made it through the first two rounds in the playoffs but again, they met the Detroit Pistons and fell in the decisive seventh game.

The following year, the Chicago Bulls finished the 1991 NBA season with the best record in franchise history. Their record was 61–21, and they *swept* their archrival Pistons 4–0 in the Eastern Conference Finals.

The Bulls then defeated the Los Angeles Lakers (led by Magic Johnson) in the NBA Finals. Michael Jordan won his second NBA MVP Award that season and his first championship.

The Chicago Bulls went on to win five more championships over the next seven years, with Phil Jackson at the helm, continuing the refinement of the *team-based* triangle offence, led by Michael's amazing talent.

From 1991–1998, the Chicago Bulls won six championships, becoming one of the greatest dynasties in sports history. Michael Jordan became, some say, the greatest basketball player—if not the greatest *athlete*—of all time.

Yet, none of this would have happened if Michael had tried to do everything himself. Sure, he may have won one or two championships. He would've had an incredible stat sheet. But he would not have emerged as a legend in one of the most dominant dynasties in sports.

Michael's true brilliance was only possible as he transformed into more of a team player, built around a team system, led by a genius coach.

There's one more thing that most people don't know about Michael, and that's that he had a private strength and conditioning coach, Tim Grover, for almost his entire career. Tim's expertise in human physiology and performance was exactly what Michael needed to exceed his own limitations and weaknesses. Michael invested huge into getting the most effective coaching and conditioning he could get, and that is a huge reason why as an individual player, he was so good for so long.

The story of Michael Jordan highlights many important insights for anyone seeking higher levels of achievement and success. However, the most crucial lesson may be that

Michael Jordan was not a self-contained entity. His "potential" was not innate or fixed, but rather, contextual and relational. Michael Jordan was literally changed and expanded through his team, coaches, and experiences. He became more than he would have become on his own, both as a person and as a talent.

Which begs the question: If Michael Jordan, perhaps the greatest and most driven athlete on the planet, needed a *Who, not a How*—first in Pippen and later in Grover and Jackson—to achieve and exceed his goals, then do you think the same could be said for you and me? What would happen for us if we, gleaning this precious insight, would shift our mind-set from "how" to "who"? What would be possible for you if your capabilities and potential were expanded by other brilliant Whos? In looking at your own life for a moment, how much of it are you trying to shoulder alone, for one reason or another?

If Michael Jordan couldn't *get to*, let alone win, a championship by himself, why would you even consider trying to pursue your goals on your own?

Now, clearly, Michael Jordan was trying to accomplish something huge. Winning one NBA championship, let alone six, is very difficult. Which leads me to the next question:

What are YOU trying to accomplish?

Do you have Whos in your life that give you the perspectives, resources, and ability to go beyond what you could do alone?

Or are you keeping your goals *so small* to make them easier to accomplish them on your own?

Do you really think you must be the one to put in the blood, sweat, and tears, bearing the whole load to prove your capability?

It can be easy to focus on How, especially for high achievers who want to control what they can control, which is themselves. It takes vulnerability and trust to expand your efforts and build a winning team. It takes wisdom to recognize that 1) other people are more than capable enough to handle much of the Hows, and 2) that your efforts and contribution (your "Hows") should be focused exclusively where your greatest passion and impact are. Your attention and energy should not be spread thin, but purposefully directed where you can experience extreme flow and creativity.

Results, not effort, is the name of the game. You are rewarded in life by the results you produce, not the effort and time you put in. All too often, there is a lack of commitment to results and an over-infatuation with "process" or "hard work."

Of course, you need to work hard.

Of course, you need to become brilliant at what you do.

But none of that matters if it doesn't translate to tangible, measurable, and *rare* results.

Michael Jordan wouldn't be considered the best of all time if he hadn't won all those championships. But in order to do that, he needed Whos. He would have become nothing close to what he became by doing it by himself, by focusing on Hows.

But this is not a book about sports.

It's a book about personal transformation and reaching the highest levels of performance and success. Put more bluntly, this is a book about producing bigger and better results in the absolute most effective way possible—in the *only* way possible.

As a culture, we've been trained to focus on "How" and to work in isolation.

But if you want to really succeed at the highest level, like Michael Jordan, you're going to need to shift from a How-mentality to a Who-mentality, regardless of your level of personal talent, commitment, or genius. It is only through teamwork and collaboration that you can achieve things you previously thought impossible. Things you can't even dream of or imagine in your present situation.

This book argues that with each ascending level of success, your ability to produce results will be more and more contingent on Whos, not Hows. By focusing on Who you work with and not How you achieve your goals, your level of accomplishment, and thus freedom, will dramatically increase in all key areas—time, money, relationships, and purpose.

If you're someone who is serious about creating results, particularly in business and as an entrepreneur, this book is going to show you the way. And unless you're already a billionaire, then you've lots of room to implement the ideas this book will teach you.

WHO NOT HOW

The originator of the *Who Not How* framework and primary author of this book—Dan Sullivan—didn't write one word you're about to read.

He didn't even see the book until it was almost done, and even then, his notes were short, and I took only some of them.

Yet, the book is better than he would have written himself—even with help. And he'll tell you it's exactly what he wanted, perfectly positioned to help his ideal reader, *you*.

How could this be?

How could the person who created and mastered a concept not be the one to write the book?

And why would he want to do it this way?

Dan was living his core premise: ***Who Not How.***

Let me explain:

Whenever you imagine a bigger and better future, there's a problem. You don't currently know *how* to achieve the goal, because it's bigger and better than your current situation and capabilities.

If you are like most people, the first thing you do when you imagine a bigger future is ask yourself: *"How do I achieve this goal?"*

Although this question seems intuitive, it's actually the worst possible question you could ask (assuming you want to be happy and successful).

Yet, this "How" question is what you've been taught to ask your whole life. Our public education system is entirely based on "How." We're taught from a young age that we need to do everything ourselves. We're taught that getting help from others is "cheating," and something we absolutely shouldn't do.

But what if you asked *a different question?*

What if the instant you had a new goal in your mind, rather than procrastinating and feeling frustrated, rather than going through the slow and lonely process of achieving your goals by yourself, you could immediately experience a surge of energy and excitement? What if you could consistently achieve bigger and more powerful results, without having to do all the work? What if you could imagine and accomplish multiple huge goals at once?

That's where *Who Not How* comes in.

A NEW AND BETTER QUESTION

If you're ready to realize a much bigger and more powerful future, then you must stop asking yourself, *"How can I accomplish this?"*

That question, although common, leads to mediocre results, frustration, and a life of regrets.

A much better question is: *"Who can help me achieve this?"*

The simplicity of this new question—*"Who can help me achieve this?"*—may deceive you at first glance. Think about this for a second:

What would happen in your life if you asked this question about everything you wanted to accomplish?

What would happen if you asked this question about everything you've been procrastinating to do?

How would your goals change if you could find people—Whos—that could help you achieve everything you wanted in your life?

How would your confidence change if you had several Whos producing the results *with you*?

How would your time be spent if you were no longer the one doing everything?

How would your income change if you could achieve all your goals, and not just some of them?

How would your sense of purpose expand if you had brilliant Whos that made your goals easier to accomplish?

How would the quality of your relationships change if you could invest more time and money into those relationships?

What if you had access to anyone you wanted to learn from or collaborate with?

Can you even imagine that?

If you can imagine that world, then you are starting to understand *Who Not How*.

"WHO" CREATES RESULTS, "HOW" CREATES PROBLEMS

Dan Sullivan is the cofounder of Strategic Coach, the number one entrepreneurial coaching company in the entire world. Dan has trained tens of thousands of the very best entrepreneurs to become even better. He helps his entrepreneurs clarify their "Unique Ability"—the activities that bring them the most excitement and energy and produce the biggest impact—and then find Whos to take care of *everything* else.

He lives his own ideas. This is why he didn't write a single page of this book. He knows that it doesn't make sense for him to do any "How" that isn't the absolute best use of his time and talents.

For every How in his life except the few activities he deems his Unique Ability, Dan finds a Who.

My name is Dr. Benjamin Hardy. I'm the writer of this book, and in that role, I'm a "Who." Each chapter is in my voice and from my perspective. Therefore, Dan will be referenced in the third person throughout. Of course, Dan is the genesis of the concepts and tools found in *Who Not How*. He provided the ideas and the amazing stories of his clients who have applied his strategies to radically grow their business and gain prosperity, freedom, and happiness.

One of my favorite ways to explain Who Not How is by telling the story of how this book came to be.

After hearing Dan's "Who Not How" presentation at a GeniusX meeting held by Joe Polish, I knew this idea had merit, and not just because Dan was so excited about it, but also because it radically simplified entrepreneurship and financial abundance, condensing success to a single statement. I felt this idea needed to become a book to reach a larger audience. I knew it could help people achieve bigger goals and break past their plateaus.

As Dan sat down after his talk, I rolled my chair over to him and whispered, "I'm completely blown away by this concept. I'd like to turn *Who Not How* into a book. What do you think?"

He smiled, thanked me, and said we would discuss it shortly. The next morning, he presented me with an Impact Filter, the one-page document he gives to his "Whos" when he has a new goal (you'll learn more about this in later).

When he presented me with this document, Dan said: "Let's do this. Here's what success looks like. Here's why this project is so important for us. Here's what we gain if we succeed. Here's what's at stake if we fail. I'm here if you need me. Go!"

Who Not How is truly that simple. You define the vision, find the Who or Whos, and let *them* create the result.

That's what real leadership is: Creating and clarifying the vision (the "what"), and giving that vision greater context and importance (the "why") for all Whos involved. Once the "what" and "why" have clearly been established, the specified "Who" or "Whos" have all they need to go about executing the "How." All the leader needs to do at that point is support and encourage the Who(s) through the process.

In the summer of 2018, after having that conversation with Dan and getting his Impact Filter, I wrote the book proposal for *Who Not How*. When I presented it to my publisher, they weren't interested. Instead, they wanted me to focus on my other book project, *Personality Isn't Permanent,* and told me that they might reconsider their decision after the publication of *Personality.*

Disappointed, I reported the bad news to Dan and his cofounder, wife, and business partner, Babs. They didn't flinch and they didn't make any fuss. "It will all work out," was their reassuring response.

Over the next year, I'd occasionally ask my editor about *Who Not How,* hoping we could get that project going. Each time, I would get the same answer: "Don't ask us about that book. Let's focus on the one you're writing."

I began to feel hopeless.

I was also feeling a sense of urgency to get the project moving. I knew Dan's and Babs's time was valuable and felt the window of opportunity to do a book with them might be passing, even with their assurances that it was not. Eventually, I came to the realization that I wasn't the only Who needed to make this book a reality.

I needed to find my own Who.

My Who turned out to be Tucker Max, the four-time *New York Times* best-selling author. Tucker had helped me edit *Personality Isn't Permanent,* and when I told him about my struggles selling *Who Not How,* he said he knew exactly what to do, and that he would help.

At a GeniusX meeting in the summer of 2019, Tucker introduced Dan, Babs, and me to Reid Tracy, the president and CEO of Hay House. That night, Tucker presented the *Who Not How* idea to Reid, who was already a huge fan of Dan's work.

Within weeks of that dinner, Tucker had not only negotiated a deal for this book with Hay House, but he also negotiated a tentative multi-book deal for Dan.

When you're trying to accomplish something challenging or difficult that you've never done before, you probably need a Who. Let me say that another way: You *absolutely* need a Who if you're trying to accomplish something new and challenging, unless you're fine not getting the result you want in the near future.

The bigger the challenge, the more essential the Who. And if you *are* the Who, as I was in this case, you'll eventually discover that as the Who, you'll also need a Who.

This lesson is abundantly clear in J. R. R. Tolkien's *The Lord of the Rings* trilogy. Frodo, a simple hobbit, was the Who tasked to take the One Ring to Mount Doom and destroy it to save Middle Earth. But Frodo couldn't accomplish such a task on his own. He needed an entire fellowship of Whos to achieve this epic quest. When the vision is important enough, the right team of Whos will come together.

Frodo's ultimate Who, though, was the loyal Sam. Without Sam, *Frodo would have failed.* In many instances, Frodo tried to go it alone. When Frodo, fearing for Sam's life, tried to leave him on the shore, Sam wouldn't allow it. He waded into the water in an attempt to reach Frodo's boat, even though he couldn't swim. He nearly drowned. Seeing his friend's commitment humbled Frodo. He realized he would need Sam by his side in order to complete his mission.

In some situations, like Frodo, you will be humbled, sometimes even to tears, by the utter commitment of your Whos. Your gratitude—for the abundance of people in your life, and also for the abundance of results and freedom you're experiencing—will often overwhelm you.

In other instances, like Sam, *you will be the Who* supporting a broader vision being led by someone else. You'll be grateful for your unique role and contribution to a vision that is not only meaningful but also transformative.

Both Frodo and Sam were each other's Who. They supported and encouraged each other to do what neither of them could even consider, let alone achieve, on their own. Through their connection, they grew as people and produced a significant result which impacted their world.

Saving Middle Earth was about the right Who, being fully supported by his Who, to do what needed to be done.

Every Who needs a Who. This includes *you!* Whatever you're trying to do, you need a Who. (I know what you're thinking . . . *this is starting to sound like a Dr. Seuss book . . . read this paragraph again!*)

This book is not for people with small goals and ambitions. It is for people who want to do extraordinary things with their lives.

If you want to get progressively bigger and better results in your life, then you'll need Whos, not Hows. You can't get insane results, like Tucker's near effortless and immediate multi-book deal, by trying to figure out How. You don't get preferential treatment with Hows, but with Whos who know what they're doing.

If you're committed to specific results, then at some point or other, you're going to have to face the truth that results are produced by Whos, not Hows.

When you're ready to get results quickly and effectively, then find the right Who. As your ambition increases, you'll need to get faster and faster at foregoing the frustration of How. Instead, you'll go straight to the Who that can get the result.

Once you're committed to the result you want, you'll find that Who. When you do find that Who, you'll see how ridiculously simple it was *for them* to produce your desired result, then you'll begin to see just how small you've been playing.

You'll begin to set bigger and bigger targets, and you'll commit to those targets faster by getting the Who that is equipped to produce the result.

DELEGATION IS NOT EXPLOITATION

"There is no limit to the amount of good you can do if you don't care who gets the credit."

—Ronald Reagan

It is critically important to understand that *Who Not How* goes both ways. Yes, Tucker, Reid, and I are Dan's Whos on this book. ·

But Dan is also a Who to each of us.

Take Reid, for example. He recently launched a business imprint for Hay House. Having the chance to do Dan Sullivan's first major book is a big deal for this imprint and for Reid. Dan is a Who helping Reid to achieve *his* goals.

Same for Tucker, whose company and process effectively helps entrepreneurs write books to grow their influence and business. Dan is a huge Who for Tucker, because through Dan's network, Tucker is able to help potentially thousands of entrepreneurs improve their business through books. Dan is a Who who helps Tucker achieve *his* goals.

More than anything, Dan serves as a mentor to me. By writing this book, I get intimate access to Dan's wisdom and his team, and through this collaboration, we get to launch incredible ideas out into the world together. Dan is a Who who helps me achieve my goals as a writer and entrepreneur.

Ultimately, *Who Not How* is about teaching you how to focus on what you can do, and then finding other Whos to do what they can do. In every "Who" relationship, you will have Whos, and you will also *be* a Who. No Who is viewed as better or more important than the other. All Whos are essential to getting the project done. There is love and respect among Whos. Each member of the team views the other as a collaborator on a shared mission, and each member wants to be a hero to the others.

"WHO" TRANSFORMS AND EXPANDS VISION

The scope of the vision or "purpose" of our goal radically expanded once Tucker got involved. This is one of the keys of Who Not How: With the right Whos in place, your vision and purpose will expand dramatically.

This is what Dan Sullivan calls *Freedom of Purpose.* Your purpose and vision expand when you have powerful Whos who can take your goals to places you couldn't have imagined yourself. Dan and I weren't envisioning a multi-book deal, but a one-book project. Our vision expanded quickly with the right Who.

The bigger the vision, the more you need Whos and not Hows. By the same token, your vision grows as you get more and better Whos involved.

When you develop collaborations, particularly with world-class talent, projects and businesses can quickly expand far beyond the initial concept. Harvard psychologist Dr. Robert Kegan has a term for this—*The Transforming Self*—and he considers it the highest form of psychological and emotional evolution.

According to Kegan, the basest form of psychological development is the *Socializing Self,* which is when a person operates out of fear, anxiety, and dependence. You don't make your own decisions. You don't have your own goals. Instead, you are simply trying to be accepted by your peers and will do anything you can to conform with them.

Above the Socializing Self is the *Authoring Self,* which is when you've gone from unhealthily dependent to a much more healthy independence. You've developed your own sense of self. You have a worldview, goals, and an agenda. However, you have a perceptual filter that you cannot see beyond. Everything you do is to confirm your bias and achieve your narrow goals. This is where most people stop in their development, highly convinced of their own perspectives and unwilling to alter those views.

The Transforming Self is different from the Authoring Self in that rather than being individualistic and competitive, it is more relational and collaborative. When at this higher level, you engage in collaborative relationships for the sake of transformation. All parties have their own perspectives, beliefs, and agendas. Yet they come together for the purpose of having their own views, and even their own identities and sense of self expand. The whole becomes new and greater than the sum of all parts.

Through collaboration, striving, growth, and connection, people can and do change. They can evolve in ways far beyond what is possible through individualistic pursuits.

In order to engage in *Transformational Relationships*, each of the involved parties must be psychologically evolved to the Transforming Self level. Kegan posits that this psychological level is achieved by less than 10 percent of all individuals and organizations.

Transformational Relationships, as opposed to Transactional ones, are entered into for the purpose of change and growth. In Transformational Relationships, all parties give more than they take. There is an abundance mind-set, and an openness to novelty and change. Rather than viewing people or services as a "cost," as in the transactional mind-set, everything is viewed as an investment, with the possibility of 10X (10 times), 100X, or even bigger returns and change.

Creating 10X or 100X results in your life and business may initially sound ridiculous, but it is fundamental to applying *Who Not How*. You need bigger goals. You need a bigger vision. As Dan says, "The only way to make your present better is by making your future bigger." Going 10X bigger in your vision, whether that be income or revenue or some other metric, forces you to get Whos involved, because the task at hand literally becomes impossible to do on your own. Those are the types of goals we encourage you to start envisioning as you read this book.

Dan fully believes in this idea and only engages in Transformational Relationships. His core motive is growth. His core focus and investment are *people*. He seeks change both in himself and the entrepreneurs he coaches. As their coach, he doesn't insulate himself from the feedback of his clients. Instead, he sees their feedback as an essential ingredient in the creation and evolution of his own ideas. As he explained to me: "I only see my part of the ideation as 50 percent. Once I've gotten the idea 50 percent formed, then it's time to test it on the audience who provide the other 50 percent. Every time I share the initial concept, I'm always surprised by the feedback and comments I get. I could never guess what they are going to say and how they are going to react. Being surprised is something I seek out, and something I very much value. I'm always surprised by what becomes of the ideas and collaborations. Being surprised regularly is what keeps me young."

I was struck by Dan's level of psychological flexibility and confidence. "Have you always been this way?" I asked.

"Not to this level. I used to hold on to my ideas much longer, trying to refine them myself before sharing them with the audience. I was far less open to having the ideas changed through feedback. It required far more courage to share the ideas back then. But I've done it so much now that my courage has been replaced with confidence."

In Dan's comments, you can see his own evolution from the Authoring Self stage to the Transforming Self stage. It's no wonder that his primary coaching focus at this point is entrepreneurial collaborations in which the highest transformations and success are possible. Even still, it takes courage to become that flexible and collaborative. It takes openness and a commitment to growth.

If you're courageous enough to pursue big goals, you'll need Whos to help you. You'll need Whos to transform your vision, giving it greater purpose and possibility than your initial thoughts could.

Like Dan, you'll need to be open to being surprised. By letting Whos take care of the Hows, the final product will actually be different, *and better*, than you initially imagined. As Kegan teaches, at the Transforming Self level, all parties know the final outcome will be *better than expected*, even if it's slightly different than the initial vision. This book is better than Dan expected it to be.

The bigger your goals become, the better the Whos you'll need.

LET THE "WHO" DO THE "HOW"

Tucker ended up serving several key roles for the creation of this book. Given his know-how in the publishing world, he served as a buffer between me and the publisher, allowing me to stay in the creative flow. He also served as the seasoned and confident sounding board for Dan and Babs, helping them keep their expectations for the process and outcome of this book realistic.

For example, Tucker once told Dan and Babs that we would likely ignore 80 percent of their comments during the creation of this book. This wasn't because their comments weren't important or intelligent, but because as the Whos, we must do *our job,* which in many instances lies beyond the scope of their perspectives and judgments. His exact quote was:

"This book is not for you. It's not for the people who work for Strategic Coach. It's not for the people in Strategic Coach. Those people get the Who Not How idea. This book is for the people who should be in Strategic Coach but aren't yet, and we have to write it for them."

I did not have the confidence, gumption, or authority to say that, or many of the other things Tucker told Dan and Babs. Instead, I would have folded to the wrong advice and not maintained the courage to be the Who I needed to be to write this book. Over and over Tucker's advice to me was the same: "Ben, the thing that would make Dan happiest is if you, as the primary Who, would fully own the How. So go own it!" To his credit, Dan said the same thing. I had asked Dan for advice on writing the book. His response was classic Dan Sullivan:

"Why would I tell you how to write this book? You're the one who writes these types of books. I wouldn't even begin to know how to advise you on this, nor would I want to."

Not only must the Who fully own the How, but they must have *complete permission* to do so.

To give me that permission, Dan told me a story about Michael Crichton, the author of the *Jurassic Park* novels. Crichton was once asked during an interview how much of his books ended up making it into the major motion picture films. Crichton explained that approximately only 10 percent of his books translated into the films.

The interviewer pushed back, "Doesn't that make you mad?"

"Not at all," Crichton replied. "Those movies sell a lot of books."

Michael Crichton's books have sold more than 200 million copies. A large portion of those sales have come from allowing Whos to take his ideas and use them in different forms. In order to do so, Crichton had to remove his ego from the equation. He couldn't force his own thinking onto other mediums and projects. He had to let people take his ideas in different directions than he would have himself. Indeed, he wasn't a film director. He wasn't a movie savant. *He was a novelist.* And he let other Whos do what they did, in their own way, and as a result, he was a *huge recipient.*

This lesson will be taught over and over throughout this book: ***If you're going to apply higher levels of teamwork in your life, you'll need to relinquish control over how things get done.***

Instead, you'll need to put your trust in capable Whos, giving them full permission to own their Hows. Only then will you get people's greatest work. As Albert Einstein has said, "Everything that is really great and inspiring is created by the individual who can labor in freedom."

TRANSFORMATIONAL LEADERS GIVE THE VISION AND GET OUT OF THE WAY

This book is not a perfect explanation of Dan Sullivan's ideas and thinking. The only way for you to access that would be for you to join Strategic Coach. But consider this the popular translation of Who Now How, just as the *Jurassic Park* movies are popular translations of Crichton's books. Although the films did not perfectly depict Crichton's books, they did lead many people back to reading the novels, where they could get an even deeper and richer experience. Such is the case with this book.

If you're an entrepreneur looking to multiply your business tenfold and create more freedom in your life, then this book contains everything you need. But if you want to take your transformation even further, then join Strategic Coach, where you can draw directly from the well that inspired this book.

A core aspect of leadership is being explicit about the vision. The more explicit you are in what you want, the faster you'll attract the right Whos to help you achieve that vision. The leader explains the "What" and "Why" and then allows the "Who" to execute the "How."

In full disclosure of our vision for this book, it is our goal to enhance the lives of every reader. We also hope that over time, at least 500 readers who recognize the power of these ideas, and who are committed to creating greater freedom in their lives, will invest big in themselves and their future by joining Strategic Coach. That is the vision Dan gave to me, as his Who. That vision is all I needed to go about executing the How.

Even with Dan's blessing and permission to be the Who, I often needed a great deal of coaching. Initiating this project was an act of courage. More than once I realized that I was in over my head. My greatest Hows couldn't get me where I needed or wanted to go.

Eventually, the message of Dan's books and teachings finally became real to me. Every time I encountered a roadblock, I needed a Who, not a How. It has taken time, and I'm still unlearning the bad habit of How, and leaning into the good habit of Who. I'm getting better and faster at going straight to Who the instant I get stuck. As I've done this, my confidence and results have increased.

The same thing can be true for you.

ARE YOU PLAYING CHECKERS OR CHESS?

NBA star Kobe Bryant once told his teammate Shaquille O'Neal, "These young guys are playing checkers. I'm out there playing chess."

Most people and entrepreneurs are playing checkers. They are focused on far too many Hows and thus stymie their own vision and self-expansion. When you learn and apply Who Not How, you'll switch from playing checkers to chess. And instead of playing someone else's game, you'll be the one designing the game. You'll determine what the objective is, and what pieces need to be on the board.

As you get better at Who Not How, you'll be able to create multiple games at once. Every goal or project you initiate starts a new game. Each game requires different pieces and players—*different Whos*. As you become a grandmaster, the games you play will become increasingly bold, profitable, and successful. You'll need increasingly valuable and powerful pieces—Whos—to be on your gameboard.

But unlike typical chess, with each game of Who Not How you play and win, your pieces will become more powerful, as will your own ability to create new strategies and get new chess pieces with enhanced capabilities.

The other key difference from chess is that you don't have opponents—in this game, virtually everyone is a potential partner. As you learn to see this, you will become bolder and more visionary, and your ability to attract and collaborate with increasingly capable Whos will grow exponentially. Consequently, your desire for more and greater teamwork will expand, and with it so will your level of freedom.

Are you playing checkers or chess?

What is the level of vision you have for yourself?

Does your game involve powerful Whos to help you win?

Do you seek to be surprised by what could happen?

HOW THIS BOOK IS ORGANIZED

In Part 1 of this book, I will show you how **Who Not How can give you more time**, because you'll no longer be considered the first or best option to complete a given task. Rather, you can "free up" more and more of your time by delegating or outsourcing all predictable Hows to other people, external companies, or even technology.

In Part 2, I'll teach you how **Who Not How can make you more money**, because when you begin enlisting "Whos" to support your growing goals, you'll no longer be distracted and focused on nonproductive activities. Making money is a confidence and leadership game, and a skill you can develop and master.

In Part 3, I'll walk you through how **Who Not How will help you cultivate more and better-quality relationships**. As you increase your standards for how you spend your time, and as your goals increase, you'll be required to surround yourself with higher level Whos. You'll need better mentors to help you get to the next level. You'll need better, more confident, and more capable employees to take on your increasingly inspiring objectives. You'll need world-class collaborators to help take your thinking and work to places that not only you, but your competitors, could never imagine.

Finally, in Part 4, I'll show you how **Who Not How helps you develop a greater and deeper sense of purpose in your life**. Your purpose is what you live for. It's why you believe you're here on this planet. It's how you define yourself. It's how you spend your time. With each application of Who Not How, your confidence and vision for your future will grow and your sense that you can make a powerful and meaningful impact will increase. You'll also find additional nuggets of wisdom from Dan sprinkled throughout the book.

The promise of this book is dead serious and simple: Every time you apply Who Not How by imagining a new goal and getting Whos to work toward it, you will improve your time, increase your income, expand your relationships, and deepen your purpose.

If you don't, you'll continue to be frustrated and to procrastinate instead of pursuing your dreams. You'll live a life of regret, becoming a shell of who you might have been. As the famous quote says: "Someone once told me the definition of Hell: The last day you have on earth, the person you became will meet the person you could have become."

Who Not How is the answer.

Are you ready?

If so, then let's begin.

PART 1:

FREEDOM OF TIME

CHAPTER 1

"WHOS" CREATE ABUNDANCE AND SELF-EXPANSION

"When the student is ready, the teacher will appear."
—Buddha

When Richie Norton was a 16-year-old boy, he really wanted to start working. Although Richie came from a middle-class family and lacked nothing, he longed for control. He wanted the freedom to make his own money and spend it on whatever he wanted, whenever he wanted. Richie figured his best option was to get a job at a grocery store or gas station. Or, perhaps, he'd be able to pick up trash at the County Fair. After having thought about it for a while, and convinced he was ready to get a job, Richie told his dad.

"I don't want you to get a job," his dad replied.

"But I want one."

"You're a kid. You're going to be working your whole life."

"But I want money."

"Okay, Richie," his dad said. "If you want money, then go to El Centro, to the watermelon farms. Ask if you can buy all of the irregular sized and shaped watermelons. The farms can't sell them, and they just end up going rotten and being thrown away."

Richie and his younger brother, Erik, took out all of the backseats in the family van and made the two-hour drive south from their hometown in North County, San Diego, California, to El Centro. The strangely shaped watermelons were super cheap, so they were able to buy enough watermelons to fill the van, top to bottom, with the "seed money" their dad gave them.

When they got home, Richie opened the neighborhood phone book and started calling down the list of potential watermelon buyers, including his friends' parents and his local community. He told them he had watermelons that were totally delicious, just oddly shaped, and that they could buy one or more from him for cheaper than they could get at the grocery store. It was just days from the Fourth of July, so he knew the refreshing fruit would be in high demand.

Within a few short hours, he had sold his entire supply of about 100 watermelons. He arranged with all of his buyers to meet at the park on a specific day at a specific time. He took the watermelons to the park to distribute them, and in a few hours, he had made more money than he would have made over an entire summer working for minimum wage.

When Richie first decided he wanted to have more money, he asked, *"How can I make money?"* This question led him to the solution of getting a job that is typical for 16-year-olds.

By asking "How?" Richie was going to give away his entire summer. "How" costs a lot of time.

Richie's dad was an entrepreneur and thought differently about time and money. When Richie talked to his dad, his dad became Richie's "Who" in showing Richie a more effective way to make money with the least amount of effort. If money is the desired outcome, then what's the most effective and simplest way for that to be accomplished?

In asking his dad for help, Richie was able to gain the perspective and access he lacked and incorporate his dad's knowledge, capabilities, resources, and solutions. He now had a Who to help him more effectively create the result he wanted. It's safe to say that Richie would never have thought of the watermelon idea on his own.

But with his dad's solution, Richie didn't have to give away months of his time and freedom. He got his desired result almost immediately. That's the power of having a Who—you instantly get access to knowledge, insights, resources, and capabilities that are not currently available to you.

"How" is linear and slow.

"Who" is non-linear, instantaneous, and exponential.

This was a turning point experience for Richie, one that has shaped the trajectory of his life. By saving his summer while at the same time getting the money he wanted, Richie determined to never sell away his time. And he never has. By saving his summer and by creating his desired result much faster, Richie radically increased his *Freedom of Time*. Like each of the four key freedoms you'll learn about in this book, Freedom of Time is not fixed, but flexible. It's not finite, but infinite. You never reach a place where you can't improve your Freedom of Time, because it isn't solely about having all the time to do what you want. It also involves using your time on increasingly quality activities.

Now in his late 30s, Richie and his wife, Natalie, live in Hawaii with their three sons. Richie works from his cellphone as an international serial entrepreneur creating products and services, and consulting for entrepreneurs and creatives, helping them get their dreams off the ground in a way that also creates more abundant time in their lives.

This *Freedom of Time* also allows Richie and Natalie to write books, foster children, travel the world, and serve others in a capacity that would have not been possible without learning from a Who.

In fact, I have benefited directly from Richie's work. I reached out to him when I was a young writer trying to get my business off the ground. We have worked together for years now, collaborating on various projects.

For Richie, Freedom of Time is as essential as air. Several years ago, one of his and Natalie's sons died, further cementing the idea in Richie's mind that time is precious and should not be taken for granted. He now lives every single day like it could be his last, and even created an acronym for time: Today Is My Everything.

Throughout this book, you'll see how people apply Who Not How in different ways—primarily in the form of employees and collaborative partners—to create more freedom in their lives. Richie's story highlights the crucial fact that you already have several Whos all around you. Your life is filled with Whos that serve specific and unique roles, enabling you to be and do what you otherwise could not.

You have a mail carrier who brings your mail.

You have friends who encourage you.

You have mentors who inspire you.

In the watermelon story, Richie's dad is a Who for him in many ways. As his father, he primarily provides Richie with love and support. He also teaches Richie how to think about time and money. But as is true in all relationships, both parties are Whos for each other. Richie is a crucial Who to his dad, giving his life deep meaning, purpose, and joy.

We all have Whos in our lives we rely on, who help us achieve our goals and support us in various ways. Likewise, *we are all Whos to other people*, providing some form of support or connection they need or want.

Think about the Whos in your life.

What would your life be like without them?

How would *you* be different without them?

By that same token, what could your life be like if you were surrounded and supported by an increasing quantity and quality of Whos?

How would your vision for your future change if you had more Whos to help you?

In the realm of business, getting specific Whos to support you in your goals is an *investment*, often requiring money. However, as Richie's story shows, not all Whos require money. It didn't cost Richie a dime to ask for his dad's advice, but it saved him three months and changed his life forever.

Who Not How is about utilizing relationships, and being transformed by them.

"All progress starts with telling the truth."

AVOIDING THE "HOW" TRAP

"You live as if you were destined to live forever, no thought of your frailty ever enters your head, of how much time has already gone by you take no heed. You squander time as if you drew from a full and abundant supply, though all the while that day which you bestow on some person or thing is perhaps your last."

—Lucius Annaeus Seneca

Like many entrepreneurs, Sharon Duncan was working "a zillion hours per week." She had no work/life balance, was trying to keep far too many balls in the air at once, and her stress levels were "through the roof." She barely had time to spend with her aging mother.

Sharon is ambitious and loves growing. She invests in herself, and as a result, she sought coaching from Dan. One of the first things Sharon learned was a concept Dan calls "Free Days," and how he and Babs spend three months every year traveling, relaxing, and not working.

When you have a Self-Managing Company of capable Whos, Dan explained, you work less but accomplish much more. In a Self-Managed Company, your Whos manage themselves; they aren't managed by you. They have full responsibility for how they handle themselves because you've made the vision abundantly clear and exciting. You've then given them full ownership over executing and achieving the vision in whatever way suits them.

In Dan and Babs's experience, your team can and should operate seamlessly without you. This should be the goal of every entrepreneur. Having freedom to relax, recover, play, or do whatever you want is crucial for entrepreneurial creativity, success, and longevity.

As it turns out, this isn't just a fancy idea. Research shows that only 16 percent of creative insight happens while you're at work. Instead, ideas generally come while you're at home or in transit, or during recreational activity. You need time and space, and most important, relaxation and recovery, to allow ideas and solutions to ferment and form.

The first Who is always yourself: Improve yourself, value yourself, and ensure that you are in optimal form—happy, creative, and connected to the most important people in your life.

Sharon loved this idea. It sunk in particularly deep because her mom was 82 years old—and who knew how long she'd be around? Sharon's mom also happened to be a huge baseball fan, which led Sharon to the idea:

"What if I freed myself up with Whos to such a degree that I could take three months off per year and spend that time traveling the country going to major league baseball games with mom?"

It seemed far too important to procrastinate any longer. When the why is strong enough, you get real. You get serious. Like Richie, who in a single instant got a perspective and solution beyond anything he would have concocted himself, Sharon now had a new perspective and solution. Even more important, she had a deeply compelling why, which gave her new perspective even more import, purpose, and context.

Sharon quickly got to work hiring what she called her "Practice Manager," whose role essentially comprised much of the work that had formerly stressed Sharon out. Looking back now, she realizes she could have freed herself of these tasks long ago, but she didn't have the insight or confidence to do so.

By adding that one role, her Practice Manager, Sharon immediately freed up 500 hours per year in her schedule. Those 500 hours are the equivalent to 12.5 40-hour work weeks, or three months of full-time work. By hiring one Who, she now had all of that time back to use in whatever way she wanted.

All she needed was a goal (a "what"), a reason (a "why"), and a Who.

In fact, the simplicity was almost shocking to Sharon. Her stress levels immediately plummeted. Her vision broadened for what her life and business could be like, and Sharon began to value her time more.

That's how confidence feels.

Since hiring her Practice Manager, Sharon and her mom have gone to countless baseball games. They even went to every single game of the 2018 World Series. They've created memories that both Sharon and her beautiful mother will never forget. Furthermore, her mom has been able to live her dream of going to baseball games with her daughter. Her mom can't even believe what she and her daughter are able to do together and will continue to do.

Sharon is now becoming the master of her time. Whatever work she engages in now must be work she is deeply passionate and excited about. It has to be the absolute best use of her time. It has to make the biggest impact on the mission and revenue of her company.

Sharon's Practice Manager, as well as the rest of her team, is thriving. Because Sharon is far more focused, energized, and excited, the company is experiencing incredible growth. Everyone feels like they are a part of something special. Everyone is feeding off their leader's energy and spirit.

Creating these types of experiences for yourself and others is priceless. And it's completely available to you, if you get serious about your time.

Time is finite. We all have 24 hours. Before you can master any of the other freedoms, you must become a master of your own time.

You can accomplish a million times more if you stop asking "How?" and start getting Whos.

> "Creators don't complain; complainers
> don't create."

"WHOS" ARE HOW YOU EXPAND AS A PERSON

According to the *Self-Expansion Model* developed by married psychologists, Dr. Arthur Aron and Dr. Elaine Aron, humans have a primary motivation for "self-expansion," which is the desire to enhance your efficacy or confidence.

From this model, "efficacy"—your ability to produce a desired result—is not viewed in absolute terms, but rather in "potential" terms. As a person, your efficacy is not about what you can solely do on your own. It's not based on your "innate" or "individual" capabilities. Rather, efficacy refers to your obtaining resources that make the attainment of your goals possible. The way you increase your potential efficacy, or self-expansion, is by creating close relationships, which in turn, increases material and social resources, perspectives, and identities.

According to the Arons, when two people enter a relationship with each other, each party incorporates and merges aspects of the other person into themselves. Psychologically, we view the other person as an integrated aspect of ourselves. The other person's resources, to some degree, have just become our own. And vice versa.

The resources you obtain through relationships can be material, like money, possessions, or friendship networks. But resources also include the other person's perspectives, such as how they appreciate the world and ascribe explanations for people's behaviors. Resources may even be their time, attention, or help.

Our motivation to expand as individuals leads us to seek close relationships with other people. Our attraction to specific people, according to the Arons, is based on two factors:

- **Desirability:** the perceived total amount of self-expansion that is possible for us through that specific relationship.

- **Probability:** the perceived likelihood that a close relationship with that specific individual can actually be formed.

What all of this tells us is that our efficacy, capability, and potential as human beings is not absolute, innate, or fixed. It is always contextual, relational, and fluid. What you can accomplish in relation to some people is very different from what you can do in relation to others. What you can learn and become with some people is different than with others.

This fact became radically clear to me when my wife, Lauren, and I became foster parents of three children. These kids came from a very limiting environment. They were neglected by their parents, not given the attention or resources they needed, and were, frankly, left in front of the television all day.

In that situation, these kids didn't have much potential. They couldn't produce results, even with their best efforts. But with a change in their environment and context, all of a sudden, they had a very different potential.

They had access to additional resources through us. This included our home and money, but also our energy and our time. We invested (and still do) a great deal into these kids. We got them private tutors, as they were all behind in school. We got them into therapy, supported their interest in sports, took them to church, and traveled all over the United States with them. They also benefited from the expanded resources of our extended families, such as loving grandparents who took them on fishing trips and cruises, and tons of cousins to play with and love. They had access to our knowledge and perspectives, and even our spiritual beliefs.

All of these additional resources and experiences transformed our children. Through tutoring they developed skills and confidence they otherwise would not have. Thus, their future learning and opportunities expanded. Through therapy, church, and close relationships, they've learned how to emotionally regulate, handle stress and anxiety, and better understand their challenges and experiences. Through travel and family experiences, as well as being surrounded by people who love them and are successful, they have better self-esteem and a higher level of goals and expectations for themselves than they had before.

The point here is, as you engage in relationships, you expand your efficacy as a person. Your efficacy is your ability to produce results, and it is based on the resources you have to put toward those results. Resources can be financial, but they can also be so much more than that. Encouragement, time, and focus are just as essential as monetary support. Resources not only expand your ability to produce results, but can have a transformational effect on you as a person—on your identity, worldview, and skill level. For instance, with the resource of a piano teacher, your skill can be enhanced to a level not possible without.

This is one of the core reasons why Who Not How is such an important mind-set shift to experience. If you're focused on doing everything yourself, then you are dramatically limiting the resources you can direct toward your goals. If your resources are limited, your potential, your options, and your future are limited too.

But as you combine your efforts with other Whos, your efficacy immediately increases. Relationships are how you transform as a person. Relationships are how you transcend your current limitations. Relationships are how you produce results. Relationships are the purpose of life.

More specifically, research clearly shows that your relationships—not your willpower—are what help you overcome something like an addiction. As writer and journalist Johann Hari famously stated in his hit TED Talk, "The opposite of addiction is not sobriety—it is human connection." Alcoholics Anonymous (AA), for many addicts, becomes an incredible resource of Whos. The "addict" is truly ready to change when they stop trying to do it solely by themselves and when they openly admit they need help, both from a Higher Power and other people.

Given all of this, it's critical that we challenge our trained response to ask "How?" when it comes to achieving our goals. Why ask How, when your motivation and efficacy have far more to do with your relationships than your perceived abilities? Why ask How, when doing so may keep you permanently stuck where you are, such as with an addiction?

You expand yourself and your efficacy through relationships!

Ultimately, anyone who becomes highly successful does so through relationships. Success becomes increasingly about Who and less about How as you grow. This fact cannot be escaped. It is for this reason that you must shift from How to Who in all that you do. If you want increased freedom in your life, you simply can't approach it by doing all the Hows.

You need Whos: spouses, parents, mentors, teachers, coaches, collaborators, co-conspirators, and eventually, when you're ready, employees and other people who work for you.

Employees, collaborators, and consultants work for you not because they are beneath you, but because they believe in you. You become an incredibly important Who in their life, giving them a mission to be part of, a way to provide for themselves and their families, and a way to build competence and confidence.

The more people you are a Who for, the more successful you will become. As motivational speaker Zig Ziglar once said, "You can have everything in life you want, if you will just help other people get what they want." Helping people get what they want doesn't mean you're doing all the "Hows," but rather, that through your resources, whatever those may be, you can enable them to get what they want and need.

Dan often says that the best way to measure your progress is by noting the amount and quality of collaborations happening in your life. According to the Self-Expansion model of psychology, this makes absolute sense. Your efficacy as a person is based on the resources you have, which are a direct by-product of your relationships. Every relationship can be viewed as teamwork, directed toward a purpose.

Take a look at your life right now:

Where are you lacking collaboration and teamwork?

Where is your vision so small that you're doing everything by yourself?

Where do you need more Whos to help you accomplish what you ultimately want to do?

What relationships do you already have that are being under-utilized?

Think broadly about this. Consider more than just your business.

Do you have Whos in your vision for your health?

What about your vision for your family?

Are there potential Whos involved in any other passions and hobbies you have?

What about your environment?

Do you have additional resources and efficacy in all areas of your life, or is your vision limited by what you can do on your own?

Getting Whos involved in your goals is an investment. Often, we lack the commitment to make such an investment. We aren't fully sold on our goals ourselves, so why would we include others in our goals? As will be shown throughout this book, it is actually the investment in Whos that strengthens your own commitment to your goals. As you get others involved, that action enhances your desire and motivation to get serious and get focused. You put yourself in a situation where you rise to a higher occasion, and where you have other people committed to helping you succeed.

For example, if you want to improve your health, you could simply get a gym membership. Or you could hire a personal trainer. Yes, this would be an investment, one you may not think you have the capacity to make. However, by hiring a personal trainer, your capabilities and potential in your health and fitness will expand. You'll be able to produce better results because you'll get the coaching and support you need.

Additionally, by being invested, you'll be more motivated and focused, not semi-committed. Again, getting Whos is how you get committed. Investing in your goals is how you grow into and achieve huge goals. Yet, people often don't make such investments, and as a result, never experience the increased commitment, motivation, and focus that comes with it.

You control your own level of commitment to your future. You control your own level of potential for expansion. By making the courageous step of investing in Whos, your capacity as a person increases. Indeed, that's what Strategic Coach is all about: providing entrepreneurs the mindsets, tools, and community to 10X or 100X their income and impact. Through the education and relationships one gets through Strategic Coach, as well as the enhanced commitment to their vision through investing tens of thousands of dollars, entrepreneurs can break through their limitations and reach new heights, thus expanding their identity, confidence, and freedom.

The question is, are you willing to invest in Whos? Are you willing to take that leap of faith and solidify your commitment to your dreams? Or, are you going to remain semi-committed? Get some skin in the game. But also, get other people's resources to help you achieve what you can't alone. Get their knowledge, time, and connections. Free yourself from having to do it all alone. Focus where it is most needed and effective. Expand yourself and your potential.

As you shift to Who Not How, you'll evolve as a person. You'll have increased self-expansion, which will transform your identity, perspectives, and resources. You'll have a growing freedom in all four key ways—time, money, relationship, and purpose.

"Our eyes only see and our ears only hear
what our brain is looking for."

CHAPTER TAKEAWAYS

- "How" limits you to your own knowledge and capabilities.

- "How" requires that you be the one to engage your time and attention into the particular task.

- "How" decreases your Freedom of Time.

- "Who" immediately connects you with different knowledge, insights, and capability.

- "Who" is about getting the desired result as effectively as possible.

- "Who" can immediately free up hundreds of hours, which you can spend in better and more meaningful ways.

- "Who" expands your vision for what is possible, because you no longer see yourself as the sole means of achieving the result.

- Self-expansion is a core human motivation, and it occurs through Whos.

CHAPTER 2

THE TRUTH ABOUT PROCRASTINATION AND HOW TO KILL IT

"You pile up enough tomorrows, and you'll find you are left with nothing but a lot of empty yesterdays."
—Meredith Willson

The sad truth is that most people spend the majority—if not the entirety—of their lives putting off the things that matter most. Research shows that between 85–95 percent of college students are chronic procrastinators—meaning they cannot get themselves to do the work they need to do, and as a result, experience negative and undesired consequences.

Although high, these numbers are actually on the rise due to widespread addiction to technology and the Internet. According to recent studies, excessive online consumption leads to procrastination and lack of motivation.

In turn, procrastination has damaging psychological impacts. Research shows that procrastination:

- Diminishes well-being
- Increases feelings of shame and guilt
- Increases symptoms of major mental health problems such as depression
- Leads to other health risks due to poor decision-making, such as failing to seek medical treatment when ill

Although these consequences for procrastination are major, they don't even scrape the surface. Procrastination will ruin your life and limit your potential. Because procrastination stops you from achieving your goals, you miss the continuous uptick in confidence that comes from making progress. As Dan has said, "Personal confidence comes from making progress toward goals that are far bigger than your present capabilities."

Confidence is belief in your ability to imagine, conceptualize, and achieve goals. It is the foundation of imagination. Meta-analytic research shows that confidence is the by-product of recent performance or recent progress toward your goals. By growing your confidence, your imagination and future will simultaneously grow as well.

Procrastination doesn't only stop your confidence from growing. You also limit your imagination, preventing you from seeking out bigger and bigger goals. Your identity or self-concept becomes limited. You stop believing you can achieve big goals, because your identity is largely shaped by your behavior. And this pattern will cause you to assume the same for your future. Thus, procrastination leads to a small self-image and an increasingly smaller future for yourself.

You stop trusting in yourself.

You stop believing in yourself.

Although these scenarios may seem extreme, they are actually accurate statements of what happens to *most* people.

Research has shown that the number one deathbed regret for most people is that *they never took steps to do what they truly wanted to do with their lives.* Instead, they procrastinated when it came to realizing their deepest dreams and settled for less.

"Your future is your property."

THE SHOCKING AND EXCITING TRUTH ABOUT PROCRASTINATION

"A man who dares to waste one hour of life has not discovered the value of life."

—Charles Darwin

So, I've sold you on the idea that procrastination is really bad, right? Here's where I throw a monkey wrench into everything: Paradoxically, **procrastination is actually a form of *wisdom*.**

Procrastination is a psychological phenomenon that occurs when you really want something more for yourself, but you lack the knowledge and capability to do it.

What procrastination means is that your goal or ambition is great. It's something you'd like for yourself, but you're not the right person to execute the plan to achieve it, at least not right now. You need a Who to get you through whatever stage you're in, because at the moment, you're clearly not the Who in possession of the needed knowledge or capability. If you were, *you wouldn't be procrastinating.*

Procrastination is wisdom—if you listen to it.

If you don't listen, then procrastination leads to misery and mediocrity.

Procrastination is a very powerful signal telling you that it's time to get another Who involved. You're stuck. You need help.

The question is: *Will you find that help or just sit by yourself?*

The bigger your personal ambition, the more procrastination you'll experience. Everyone who is ambitious procrastinates. It is part of having big goals that stretch far beyond you.

But for most people procrastination never leads to creating the result. Instead, it leads to inaction, regret, and frustration. And once there is a lack of progress and confidence, soon ambition is lost altogether.

You only have two options when you procrastinate. The first and most common approach is to ask yourself, *"How do I do this?"* This generally leads to more procrastination. "How?" is the question society and our public education system have trained us to ask the moment we have a goal or desire.

The second, and more effective option, is to simply shift the question to, *"Who can help me with this?"* By doing so, you can stop procrastinating and feeling discouraged. Instead, you can experience an injection of energy, confidence, and creativity.

Another powerful variation of this question could be, "Who can achieve this goal *for* me?"

Who has the skills, knowledge, connections, and expertise to get this done ASAP?

Asking "Who?" is the automatic response you need to develop every time you think of a new goal or desire.

By asking this new and better question, you'll start to make immediate progress toward even your biggest goals. You'll have access to someone else's time, knowledge, connections, and capability. You'll stop being limited by yourself.

Applying Who Not How, and thus killing procrastination, requires two essential steps:

- Be radically explicit about your goals.
- Ask yourself: Who can help me accomplish this goal?

#1: BE RADICALLY EXPLICIT ABOUT YOUR GOALS

"When you speak of what you want, and even one person hears, it may begin a generative loop."

—Joshua Wolf Shenk

Lars Ulrich moved to Orange County, California, when he was in high school. At the time, he was obsessed with the new wave of British heavy metal, which included bands like Saxon, Iron Maiden, and Def Leppard.

Ulrich stood out like a sore thumb in his high school, where, according to Ulrich, there were 500 kids wearing pink Lacoste shirts while he was the one guy in a Saxon T-shirt. He was an outsider, doing his own thing. People looked at him like he was from another planet.

Ulrich felt so isolated that he took out a classified ad in the local paper, *The Recycler*. His ad was simple: Drummer looking for other musicians to jam with. James Hetfield answered the ad.

Upon their first meeting, Hetfield was so shy that he wouldn't make eye contact. But they shared the same passion for music. Together, they co-founded a band called Metallica, which went on to sell more than 100 million albums.

It all started because Ulrich knew what he wanted, he put his desire on paper, and his goal attracted the right Who. But this was back in the 1970s before the Internet and smartphones and search engines. Ulrich used the newspapers to share his vision and attract a Who. Today we have far more powerful tools and can access Whos from all over the world to help us achieve our goals.

The first thing we must learn then is to clearly define what we want. Ulrich wanted to play music with other musicians. That was his goal.

In order to create the right types of relationships, you need to be very clear about what you want. Not only do you have to know what you want, but you must clearly communicate your desires to others.

Lars Ulrich clearly said what he wanted. He expressed his desire, put it out there, and the right Who, James Hetfield, raised his hand. Had Ulrich not been explicit and vocal about what he wanted he would have never met Hetfield. They would have never transformed together and created Metallica. They would have never raised their vision and sold more than 100 million albums.

Ulrich needed Hetfield, and Hetfield needed Ulrich. Without Ulrich's ad, what would have happened to Hetfield?

The "right" Who is always ready and waiting. All you need to do is express your vision clearly.

In psychology, the term "selective attention" describes the idea that as humans, we have an incomprehensible amount of data coming into our brain through our senses. However, our conscious mind filters the information and pays attention to the things that seem relevant or important. It is for this reason that when you buy a new car you start seeing the same model everywhere or why you can hear your name in the sea of noise in a loud room.

Dan has a really good quote that captures the power of selective attention: "Your eyes only see and your ears only hear what your brain is looking for."

When you've defined what you want—and are very clear on all of the criteria for success—then you've got something that you can not only visualize but *communicate*. As you communicate what you want to the world, your vision will crystalize, and like the one car you can easily spot among the hundreds, you'll be able to find the right Whos. *Indeed, the right Whos will find you.*

Dan has created a tool that helps to define the vision, what successful completion of the project looks like, and why it is so important. He calls this tool the ***Impact Filter.***

By clarifying the vision and its importance, Dan is able to give the relevant Whos the needed information to go and successfully execute. Far too often, the Who lacks critical clarity not only about the overall vision, but about their role in that vision. Therefore, they can't bring their available resources to the table. Or, they can't find other Whos who have the needed resources.

The Impact Filter, as a one-page document, solves this most pervasive leadership conundrum, and is comprised of the following questions:

- What is the project?
- **Purpose:** What do you want to accomplish?
- **Importance:** What's the biggest difference this will make?
- **Ideal Outcome:** What does the completed project look like?
- **Best Result:** If you do take action?
- **Worst Result:** If you don't take action?
- **Success Criteria:** What has to be true when this project is finished?

THE **IMPACT FILTER**™

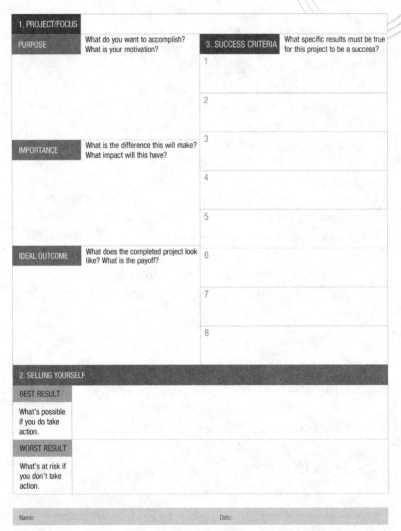

1. PROJECT/FOCUS			
PURPOSE	What do you want to accomplish? What is your motivation?	**3. SUCCESS CRITERIA**	What specific results must be true for this project to be a success?

1

2

IMPORTANCE	What is the difference this will make? What impact will this have?

3

4

5

IDEAL OUTCOME	What does the completed project look like? What is the payoff?

6

7

8

2. SELLING YOURSELF

BEST RESULT	
What's possible if you do take action.	
WORST RESULT	
What's at risk if you don't take action.	

Name: Date:

You can access and download the Impact Filter at Strategiccoach.com/whonothow.

As a rule, most people do not take the time to 1) clarify their goals or 2) adequately explain their goals. Rather than being explicit about their aims, it is common for people to keep those to themselves. By answering the Impact Filter questions, you'll be equipped to explain to other people what you want, and why it is so important. Being able to articulate and express your goals is one of the most import- ant and fundamental skills necessary for success. Only when your goal is clearly defined and persuasively expressed can you start getting the support you need to achieve your goals.

To put it more bluntly, it is actually impossible not to attract incredible Whos once your vision is defined and expressed. There is endless talent and skill—*endless resources*— waiting to be directed toward your clearly and powerfully expressed goals. People are attracted to purpose and are looking for something meaningful to be a part of. Everyone wants a compelling cause. Your vision helps your Whos, and, in turn, you become their Who, helping them achieve their vision and goals with you.

Every time you have a new goal to achieve, or have a specific project you want done, complete the one-page Impact Filter to clarify your thinking, define the vision, and ultimately, find the right Whos to execute the vision. If the Impact Filter is done well, meaning you've clearly explained what successful completion looks like, then it will be obvious to the right Who that they are the one for the job.

2: ASK YOURSELF: "WHO CAN HELP ME ACCOMPLISH THIS GOAL?"

Now that you've clarified and become explicit about your goal, you must refrain from trying to figure out "How" to accomplish it. This may be a new practice for you. If you're not used to finding Whos, you may need to muster up the courage to do so. You'll try to convince yourself why other people may not want to get involved. You may think you can't afford the right Whos, or that you're not a great leader. All sorts of limiting beliefs will flood through your mind, trying to get you to focus on the Hows, not the Whos.

Without question, it takes courage to tell people your vision. It takes courage and leadership to get other people involved. Dan often says, "The purpose of the Impact Filter is first to sell yourself on the vision, because you can't sell other people unless you're sold yourself."

So, are you sold?

Do you really want what you say you want?

Is this vision nonnegotiable?

Is it that important?

The Impact Filter you just filled out should define the importance of this project, and what you stand to gain if you succeed, and what's at stake if you fail.

Are you clear on these things?

If you're clear, and if this goal or project really matters, then are you going to be courageous?

Are you going to find Whos to support you?

Are you going to add their resources to yours, and thus *expand yourself* and your efficacy?

The crazy truth, which you may not realize yet, is that you absolutely can get Whos to help you. There are plenty of incredible and capable people who want to and will help you. All you need to do is tell them your vision. Spell it out for them. The Impact Filter actually does that for you. Then ask yourself: *"Who can help me accomplish this goal?"*

Once you've identified the needed person to help you accomplish your goal, it's time to get that person engaged and executing the needed Hows. In order to do so, you'll need to ensure your vision also matches their vision for themselves, and that you can clearly become a powerful Who to *them*. If you can, and if helping you achieve your vision will help them simultaneously become who they want to be, then you've got your Who.

Unless you're brilliant at finding Whos, you should probably find a Who to find your Whos. For example, my executive assistant, Whitney Bishop, is a pro at finding, screening, and hiring people.

Whenever I increase my vision for my future, I complete an Impact Filter to clarify that vision. I then determine the needed Who or Whos to achieve that vision. Then I give that Impact Filter to Whitney, who takes it and goes about searching for and finding Whos who are attracted to the vision and raise their hand to indicate they want to do the job. These Whos perceive themselves as having the needed resources to expand our team's efficacy.

There are endless Whos out there. No matter what "job" you put out there, you will find a Who that wants the job. Indeed, there are many qualified Whos who have the very resources you need to achieve your goal. They want to be a part of what you're doing. Moreover, they genuinely love doing the things you either can't do or don't want to do.

By working with you, they bless your life, and you bless theirs. You get their resources, and they get yours. They become your Who, and you become theirs.

For instance, Whitney would not be the same person she is now if I hadn't hired her. She not only makes a great income and supports her family, but as the leader of my team, she has developed skills she might never have otherwise cultivated. She's read dozens of books she would not have read. She told me and the other members of the team that this job has changed her life.

Likewise, it's interesting to reflect on who I would be without Whitney. She has totally transformed my business.

She has taken so much stress from my life that used to be there. She's the one who has built my team, trained them, and runs the show. Without her, my goals would not be as big and exciting as they are now.

That's pretty amazing, if you think about it. There is an army of ready and willing Whos; capable people out there who want to do the very work you need done. All you need to do is communicate your vision to those people and define what successful completion looks like. As you develop relationships with them, you'll expand as a person, immediately having greater ability to produce your desired results.

After I've given Whitney the Impact Filter, she goes through her *own* process of gathering applicants for a particular job and deciding which ones are the best fit. She has criteria, such as what traits and skills are needed for the particular role, how she feels about the candidate, and if she personally would like working with them.

I'm not entirely sure of her process for hiring because it's *her* process, not mine. That's part of the magic, I don't need to do it because I don't want to do it. I'm not the Who for that job. Therefore, I would never tell Whitney "How" to do this. She's brilliant at it and loves doing it.

That's one of the biggest mistakes entrepreneurs and leaders make: micromanaging their Whos and insisting that they do their jobs in a particular way, when the only thing that matters is the end result. Once success has been defined, restrain yourself from needing to know or care "How" it gets done. Your only concern should be that it gets done.

Let your Who do their How.

If you don't have a Whitney, then you need to put out your vision statement everywhere you can, particularly places where people are looking for jobs. But don't be afraid to share your goal or Impact Filter on social media. By sharing your goals and vision, you'll often be surprised where you can get the help you need (that's how I found Whitney).

"Having a capability is not an obligation to use it."

CHAPTER TAKEAWAYS

- People waste a large portion of their lives procrastinating.

- Procrastination is the by-product of having a goal and asking "How?" instead of "Who?"

- Procrastination has many negative effects, such as decreased well-being, frustration, and ultimately, a loss of ambition.

- Paradoxically, though, procrastination is actually wisdom. It is your inner genius saying, "This goal is amazing! But you're not the one to do everything involved!"

- Leadership involves being clear and explicit about the vision.

- The Impact Filter is a one-page tool for defining the vision or goal and why it is so important for all Whos involved.

- Asking *"Who can help me achieve this?"* may be a stretch if you've never truly committed to huge goals.

- There are countless brilliant and capable Whos out there waiting and wanting to help you. They need only to hear and understand your vision.

CHAPTER 3

FIND WHOS FOR ALL ASPECTS OF YOUR LIFE

Paul Heiss is the founder and president of IBCC Industries, Inc., a metal casting company based in China that employs more than 700 people. For decades, IBCC Industries has provided value to clients by turning scrap metal into parts for trucks, tractors, and highly engineered mechanical machinery.

However, on April 1 of 2018, everything changed. In direct retaliation against taxes approved by President Donald Trump on imported steel and aluminum, China's Customs Tariff Commission increased the tariff rate on pork products and aluminum scrap by 25 percent.

This was huge news for IBCC Industries. Over 60 percent of their clients were based in the United States, and their company, including their three operating factories, were based in Shanghai. Overnight their shipping costs skyrocketed. How were they going to get the parts their clients needed back in the United States reasonably?

Many of the world's largest manufacturing companies of construction equipment, such as Caterpillar, rely on IBCC industries for their parts. Following the passing of the tariff on April 1, Heiss began getting tons of phone calls from very concerned clients who needed to remain competitive with other companies, many of whom were based in Europe, Japan, and other parts of the world that were unaffected by the tariff.

In this heated state of affairs, it struck Heiss that he might need to move his manufacturing to India. For several years, India had been on his mind as a "someday maybe." But now, someday was *today*. His clients desperately needed him, and he had to make a move fast.

Heiss's first question was, *"How do we start manufacturing in India?"* After a few moments of confusion, he stopped his thought process. He knew that was the wrong question to ask if he was serious about getting the best and fastest results. He'd been trained by Dan, so he asked a much better question: *"Who can help me start manufacturing in India?"*

Heiss then created an Impact Filter detailing the attributes of a person he would need to fill this newly created role of "country manager." Among other things, this person needed to be:

- A native Indian
- Experienced in doing international business
- Experienced and knowledgeable about the manufacturing business

At the time, IBCC had no Indian employees, so Heiss then assigned one of his assistants to use the Impact Filter he'd created and find this country manager.

In the meantime, another immediate question came to Heiss's mind: *"Where would we build the manufacturing plants?"*

There were tens of thousands of potential locations throughout India at which to build his manufacturing plants. It would take him thousands of hours to filter through the options, and even then, he would have tons of blind spots due to his own ignorance.

He quickly realized that, again, he was asking the wrong question. He needed a Who, not a How. Time was of the essence, and he was committed to getting the best possible result. So, he asked a better question: *"Who can help us find the right lots on which to build these plants?"*

Heiss then contacted the Indian consul general, who connected him to a leader in industrial development in India. That leader did the filtering process for Heiss and then presented a small list of "best options," which Heiss then used to make his final decision.

He was able to get that list within a matter of days, not the months or years it would have taken him to attempt such a task himself. He didn't have years; he needed the best outcome for himself and his clients *immediately.*

Once he decided where the factories would be built, he was faced with another challenge: *"How do I find good suppliers of scrap steel in India?"*

By this time, he caught himself almost before he finished the question, and switched it again: *"Who can supply us with good scrap steel in India?"*

Heiss quickly discovered that there were tens of thousands of potential suppliers throughout India. Just like the location of the plants, this was an essential decision. The quality of the work they do at IBCC is based on the quality of materials they use. Going through even 100 of these potential suppliers to determine the best quality would be an enormous project. Rather than attempting to figure out how to pick the right supplier, Heiss knew he needed a Who to find the supplier for him.

Heiss was then connected to the past president of an Indian supply company who had recently retired. Heiss hired this expert as a consultant, gave him the description of the parts they made, and was soon given a short list of the optimal suppliers. Heiss then traveled to various locations to make the decision himself as to which supplier would be best. All of this allowed Heiss to move forward aggressively and get operational in a different country fast. Instead of trying to do all of those tasks himself, Heiss teamed up with Whos and was operational in India in only five months. This was absurdly, even superhumanly, fast.

But Who Not How is about results, not an obsession with "process." Allow your Whos to worry about the How and trust them to achieve the desired result within the designated timeframe. Don't micromanage their process. Let them do what they do because they are the experts, not you.

By December 2019, just 18 months after the April 1, 2018 tariff, IBCC Industries was producing more than $20 million in revenue through its factories in India, which is almost 25 percent of the company's total revenue.

Given the enormous confidence Heiss has built through this transition, and the new teams he has formed, he now knows he can expand much further and faster than he previously did in the past. *If I can do what I just did in five months, what else could we accomplish?* he wondered. *How much bigger could we grow?* His mind was racing with the possibilities. The future seemed endless. Who Not How was his ticket.

Not only has Heiss's company become more agile and capable, but he himself is more confident. Because of this experience, he's now increasingly convinced of the power of finding Whos and building teams to quickly accomplish big and challenging tasks. All he needs to do is clearly articulate his vision. He or one of his assistants then needs to find the relevant Whos that can effectively and efficiently get the job done. As he enthusiastically told me:

"I now realize that my potential is virtually limitless when I focus on Who instead of How. My goals are not constrained by me. There are endless Whos out there and I can add that capability to anything I'm trying to accomplish."

"Creative people are always inventing their past, present, and future."

FIND WHOS FOR ALL ASPECTS OF YOUR LIFE

"What is the ultimate quantification of success? For me, it's not how much time you spend doing what you love. It's how little time you spend doing what you hate."

—Casey Neistat

For years, Tony Caldwell had wondered, *"How can I eat better?"* But he couldn't get himself to do it until he learned to ask himself a different question. Then Tony switched his question to: *"Who can help me eat better?"*

This shift was revolutionary for Tony. It led to lines of thinking not available within the framework of his former question and mind-set. He decided a personal chef could help him eat better. Still, he didn't want to go through the aggravating process of finding a personal chef. He was a busy man with lots to do. Given his overall responsibilities, something simple like finding a personal chef felt like quite the undertaking.

So, he procrastinated for a while. But he really wanted to eat better. His why was becoming deep enough that he was no longer willing to tolerate feeling bloated, inflamed, and unhealthy. He wanted to be vital, feel incredible, and look better. He became fed-up enough about his lack of results to shift what was happening. He realized his question and "How" focus was getting in the way of his result. He changed his question from *"How can I find and hire a personal chef?"* to *"Who can help me find and hire a personal chef?"*

Within 30 seconds of asking that question, he thought of someone on his team who could help him find the chef. He asked her for help, and she happily said, *"Yes, I can help you with that."* In days, Tony had a chef cooking for him and his family five days a week. He didn't have to do anything.

No stress whatsoever.

By simply asking a different question—focused on Who instead of How—Tony was immediately able to solve his problem. Or better yet, have someone *else* solve his problem.

Tony now applies Who Not How broadly and deeply to all areas of his life. He seeks personally to improve both his own as well as his family's lives and time. He wants more healthy food for himself and his family, as well as more enjoyable and present experiences together.

Professionally, Tony is an insurance agency developer in the insurance distribution space. He was near retirement, but once he started asking "Who?" in all dimensions of his business, he was able to offload everything he was previously doing to various Whos within his company.

As a result, he decided not to retire. "I get to refocus and repurpose, instead of retire," he said. "It's almost like I have a whole new life given back to me."

With Tony now in a more visionary role, his team was able to double their forecasted revenue over the next three years. In other words, they were already ready and capable of flying. They just needed Tony to stop doing all the Hows and have the time and space to dream up a bigger future for the company. He now inspires and supports his team from a distance, and finds incredible opportunities he couldn't previously see to invest in.

To focus on the bigger vision, Tony applies Who Not How. For Tony, shifting his question from "How?" to "Who?" was like walking out of a dark room into the light. Rather than asking, *"How are we going to do this?"* he asks, *"Who are we going to get, either internally or externally, to make this happen?"* All of sudden, everything became possible that hadn't been before. He's now pursuing bigger projects. He's also radically opening up his calendar for the personal things he's been delaying for too long.

Recently, he gave the responsibility of his e-mail to his assistant, which initially was a challenge and transition for his assistant. But she's gotten onboard, and over time, she's taken ownership, expanded her opportunities and responsibilities, and become more capable and successful as a result.

By no longer dealing with e-mail (and other lower-level tasks or decisions), Tony has far more time. One of the things he's put off for years is flying his airplane. He simply hadn't before because, from his perspective, it required being able to get up and leave for a few weeks at a time, which he hadn't previously been able to do.

He now has the time and the freedom, because he's utilizing Whos rather than putting irrational pressure on himself to figure out Hows. Instead of being stressed and burned out at work, Tony now spends considerably more time flying his plane, sometimes taking weeks off to fly, have fun, and recover.

Within 90 days of hearing the Who Not How concept at a Strategic Coach meeting, Tony had freed up thousands of hours of current and future time by finding Whos to take care of things he used to do. Here's what Tony told me:

"It's getting a little harder to find more time to free up, since I've basically freed up everything. But I'm still thinking a lot about it. I've got a list of about two hundred or three hundred hours of tasks I still want to assign, so I'm asking myself, 'Okay, how can I get rid of this stuff?'"

Will you stop tolerating the wasteful and painful use of your time?

How you spend every second on this planet matters. You get in life what you tolerate.

You can start small. Each small win builds confidence and an increased sense that you can create the life you want. Start by simply eliminating all tasks or distractions that are unnecessary to your future self. Often, we engage in tasks simply out of habit. If it can be eliminated altogether, then eliminate it. Your future self will thank you.

"Isolation is fertile ground for hallucination."

EVERY 90 DAYS, MAXIMIZE YOUR TIME AND MAKE HUGE PROGRESS

It took Paul Heiss five months to make the transition from China to India. It took him 18 months to add $20 million of revenue through the new India plants. Although incredibly fast, because of his use of Who Not How, it still took some time to make the progress he wanted.

You can't achieve massive goals in a day. Some of your goals may be so big that they take years to achieve. Even still, you can make massive *progress* every 90 days. Breaking down your goals into 90-day increments is good for focus and motivation. By chunking down your goals into smaller steps, you can focus more directly on what is right in front of you. You can make tangible and short-term progress, and then look back every 90 days and measure tangible progress. This gives a sense of movement and momentum.

Dan has developed a process that he calls the *Moving Future*, which helps people maximize their time every 90 days. Interestingly, though, the Moving Future actually starts by having you reflect on what you've accomplished over the past 90 days. This helps you get a sense of movement and momentum.

Here are the questions on the one-page Moving Future process, which will help you improve your time every 90 days:

- Looking back over the past quarter, what are the things you have achieved that make you the proudest?

- What are the current areas of focus and progress that make you the most confident?

- Looking ahead at the next quarter, what new developments, projects, or goals are giving you the greatest sense of excitement?

- What are the five new "jumps" (progress) you can now achieve that will make your next 90 days a great quarter regardless of what else happens?

Every 90 days, as you become more intentional and better with your time, you'll accomplish more. You'll be able to reflect back and be shocked by how much you achieved. You get to enjoy the progress you're making. And every 90 days, your excitement about your future will grow.

Every 90 days, you can eliminate tasks for yourself by adding Whos to better handle the Hows. As you make progress every 90 days, your confidence will grow. Your vision will grow. Your desire to add more Whos will grow.

Answer the questions above from Dan's Moving Future process to clarify what projects or goals you want to accomplish over the next 90 days. Then ask yourself, *"Who can help me accomplish this?"*

Challenge: Add at least one Who to your goals in the next 90 days in whatever area of your life you choose. By adding a Who, your commitment will increase and your behavior will improve. As a result, your confidence that you can achieve bigger results in that particular area will improve over the next 90 days.

"It's more satisfying to be useful now than to be remembered later."

CHAPTER TAKEAWAYS

- Your potential is virtually limitless when you stop asking "How?" and start asking "Who?"

- When you ask "Who?" you can create results 10X or even 100X faster than if you ask "How?"

- You can apply Who Not How both personally and professionally.

- You can free up thousands of future hours by finding Whos.

- By freeing yourself up from Hows, you'll have a reborn sense of purpose and clarity. You'll feel like you've been given another life to live.

- Every 90 days, you can free up your time, energy, and focus by getting Whos to support your ambitions in all aspects of your life.

PART 2

FREEDOM OF MONEY

CHAPTER 4

TIME CREATES MONEY

"Efficiency is doing things right. Effectiveness is doing the right things."
—Peter Drucker

In 1997, Dean Jackson moved from Toronto to Orlando. In Toronto, he had been a real estate agent, but he decided to partner with a friend, Joe Stumpf, to create a coaching business to help real estate agents. One week per month, Dean would fly to wherever they were holding a coaching event. The rest of the month, he worked from home.

When Dean got to Orlando, he hired Mandy to clean his condo once per week. It dawned on Dean that, potentially, Mandy could do more than just clean the house. "What if she could do everything needed to have the house 'one-week ready'?" he wondered. As in, have the house and car cleaned, the laundry done, the fridge stocked—everything the condo needed for a full week.

Dean asked Mandy if she would be interested in taking on those additional responsibilities. In exchange, Mandy was given an increase in pay and Dean has also highly recommended her to several others. She agreed, and immediately, all of Dean's house needs were taken care of. Every week, it was as though the condo "reset," and had everything it needed. Clean car, clean house, clean laundry, full fridge.

He didn't have to think about any of that anymore. His time, and therefore his mind, had just experienced an upgrade in freedom, which led to a dramatic increase in his earning capacity. Mandy was an absolutely incredible Who for Dean. Likewise, Dean was a Who for Mandy. She liked the flexibility and income of cleaning houses, and Dean was a kind and long-term client for Mandy.

By investing in Whos you not only utilize their time and resources, but also free yourself up to focus your time and attention on your most high-value activities. In turn, your earning capacity improves. This is Freedom of Money. You can't improve your money freedom without increasing the Whos in your life. Freedom of Money is also about having the money you need to solve whatever problem you have. As you'll learn in Chapter 6, if you have enough money to solve a problem then you don't have a problem.

After this experience, and over time, Dean defined what he wants for his life. Here's a list that Dean devised to track his Freedom of Money.

I Know I'm Being Successful When:

1. I can wake up every day and ask, "What would I like to do today?"

2. My passive revenue exceeds my lifestyle needs.

3. I can live anywhere in the world I choose.

4. I'm working on projects that excite me and allow me to do my best work.

5. I can disappear for several months with no effect on my income.

6. There are no whiny people in my life.

7. I wear my watch for curiosity only.

8. I have no time obligations or deadlines.

9. I wear whatever I want all the time.

10. I can quit anytime.

This is Dean's definition of success, and it has led him to finding Whos for nearly every aspect of his life. Years later, he still has Mandy taking care of all his house needs. Lilian, his main administrative assistant, takes care of his business needs. All the paperwork, e-mails, phone calls, bills, and Dean's calendar go through Lilian.

Stewart is Dean's chief operations officer. Whenever he has a new idea, Dean tells Stewart, whose responsibility it is to take Dean's idea and turn it into a reality. Stewart is the leader of the actual team, and he determines who on the team is needed for the projects Dean thinks up.

All of these people (and more) are Whos for Dean, helping him create freedom and success in his life. Likewise, Dean is a Who for all of his Whos, helping them achieve their own goals.

Dean is the one who coined the "Who Not How" term, while Dan has expanded and refined it. He and Dan have a podcast called *The Joy of Procrastination*, where they discuss entrepreneurship and freedom. From Dean's perspective, there are two types of problems in business: **technical** and **adaptive.**

Technical problems are when the answer is already known. You just need to find out how to do it. For example, if you want to set up a WordPress website, that is a technical problem. There are tutorials, YouTube videos, and businesses out there that can help you solve that problem. With any technical problem, it's optimal to ask, *"Who can do this for me? Why? Because if you ask, "How can I set up this blog?"*

then you're creating for yourself an enormous and long-term commitment. As Dean explains:

"As an individual, your time and attention are linear and finite. You only have so much. So, when you ask yourself, 'How?' then *you* have to be the one to find out where to learn, *you* have to be the one to actually learn how to do it, and once you've learned how to do it, then *you* have to be the one to actually do the task for the unforeseen future. If at some point in the future, you decide to hire someone to do it for you, then *you'll* have to train them."

Dean believes time is very important, but actually sees *attention* as the crown jewel. Your attention is always 100 percent engaged in something, even if that's distraction. The problem with asking "How?" is that you're basically telling yourself, "I'm willing to spend my finite attention on this task—finding out how to learn it, learning it, actually doing it, and one day, maybe, training someone else on how to do it." This line of thinking negatively impacts how you spend your time, which directly impacts your *Freedom of Money.*

Freedom of Money occurs as you direct your time and attention toward higher impact activities. You can have way more money if you commit to having more money. You do that by investing in Whos to relieve your previous attention from so many tasks, allowing you to place your attention and energy in places that will directly increase revenue.

So then ask yourself: Do you really want to engage your attention on *this* task? Could you spend your time in better, more exciting ways? Could you find a Who to do this for you—someone who *wants* to do it, and would see you as their Who if you gave them the opportunity?

When you ask "Who?" you instantly up-level your capability and freedom. Dean looks at Whos like a utility belt. Every time you add a Who to take care of a task, you instantly add skills to your belt, such as WordPress blog capability.

"How" requires *your* time and attention.

"Who" requires someone else's.

Unlike technical problems, adaptive problems do not have a known answer, according to Dean. Because they don't have a known answer, they require a *creator*. That's where *you* are the "Who." Everything that has ever been invented or innovated was done by a Who, acting as a creator, solving an adaptive problem.

Dean chose to create products, coach people, and do podcasts because, for him and his business, these are adaptive problems. No one else would say what Dean would say, think what Dean would think, or analyze the way Dean would analyze. He's the only one with direct access to his own brain and vision, so he engages in tasks that only he can do. He gets Whos for everything else.

"The most useful thing you can do for other people is appreciate their value."

FREE UP YOUR MIND AND ENERGY BY DOING WAY LESS

"Civilization advances by extending the number of operations we can perform without thinking about them."
—Alfred North Whitehead

"Once I made a decision, I never thought about it again."
—Michael Jordan

Jacob Monty is a labor and immigration attorney in Houston, Texas. Over the past 10 years, he has stopped doing many of the tasks he once thought he had to do.

One of those tasks is driving. When Jacob learned that Dan rejected the idea of driving in 1994 so he could instead focus his time and attention on other things while in cars, Jacob was inspired.

Jacob hired a driver, and as a result, he stopped being late for meetings. He stopped feeling stressed out. He also showed up far more prepared during his meetings, because rather than driving, he would prepare for his meetings *while commuting*.

Since the creation of Uber, Jacob has used it to travel everywhere he goes. For him, the time he spends in a car is far better utilized working or being on the phone than driving. Not only does Uber save Jacob around 90 minutes per day, during which he can do higher-quality tasks, but it also improves the overall quality of his life. He's not in a hurry or late when he gets to his destination. He no longer wastes his time looking for parking spots or running through parking lots.

He simply gets dropped off right at the door where he needs to go.

His stress levels are far lower than they were before. His thinking is crisper and more focused when he steps into his high-stakes meetings. His mind-set and energy are better. His meetings are far more impactful, his leadership more effective. He's successful and, overall, just happier.

By spending around $50 on an Uber and easily finding a Who for the task of driving, Jacob is able to create 10X the impact in his meetings, which for him, is often worth tens or even hundreds of thousands of dollars.

Jacob uses his 90-minute commute to prepare for meetings, which makes the meetings more effective and creates bigger opportunities. But often, he's not preparing for a meeting, but thinking deeply about *something else*, like envisioning new projects, or reaching out to prospective clients or collaborators. In freeing up his time, Jacob also *freed up his mind*. And with a freed-up mind, he's able to create opportunities that generate increasingly large sums of money.

In psychology, there is a concept known as *decision fatigue*. What it means is that, having lots of things on your mind and weighing decisions can really exhaust your energy and willpower. Even small stressors, like finding a parking spot or worrying about being late for a meeting, can tax your mind.

When you free yourself up from various tasks, you not only free up your time, but perhaps more important, you *free up your mind* to go to different places. With a freed-up mind, you can begin creatively expanding your vision. You can seek new opportunities not previously considered. You can invest in education, mentorships, or collaborations.

Jacob freed up his mind from the many decisions involved in driving. Rather than dealing with stop signs, traffic lights, etc., he hired a Who to make those decisions for him. While those decisions were being made by someone else, Jacob's mind could focus where he wanted it to.

What about you?

Right now, your mind is locked up with whatever you are presently thinking about.

Until you free up your time, your mind will be caged. When you free up your time, you free up your mind. With a free mind, your thinking will go to a higher level. You'll have a greater belief in yourself. You'll entertain new and better thoughts. You'll have the time and energy to focus on self-improvement and further education, honing your skills and your craft. You'll have the time to work on innovating or expanding the vision or your services.

Freeing your mind isn't just about thinking. It's about having the energy to show up and perform great work, because the stage has already been set for you, not *by* you.

Rather than spending your time doing all the Hows, you can use that time, and the freedom of your mind, to master your performance. When you show up, you'll be fresh. You'll be prepared. You'll have the bandwidth and focus to become "world class" or incredible at what you do. As you become successful the demands on you will increase, and then you'll need Whos to handle as well as shield you from most of those demands, or you'll get overrun and bogged down.

High performance and continued development of skills requires intensity of focus and what psychologists call "flow," which is pure absorption in what you're doing. Flow states can become increasingly difficult to produce as one becomes more successful. What got you here won't get you there. In order to continue growing at each successive level, you need Whos to handle the increasing complexity you create as your work and influence reaches more people.

Beyond keeping you out of flow, making lots of decisions exhausts your willpower and ultimately drains your vision. Having Whos take care of most of the major and minor details will give you the space you need. With that space, your vision will expand. With an expanded vision, your quality of life and income will soar, just as they did for our friend Jacob, who threw in the towel on driving. His stress levels plummeted, his focus sharpened, and his income rose. So can yours, *when you begin investing in Whos.*

Do you want a freed-up mind or a caged one?

What would happen in your life if you made the single decision to add a Who rather than deal with the decision fatigue resulting from juggling a myriad of details? The longer you wait to invest in Whos, the more limited your thinking will be.

Relieving decision fatigue became very real to me when I applied Who Not How. When I launched my first book, *Willpower Doesn't Work*, I did everything by myself. I scheduled all my media and podcasts. I worked directly with the publisher. And after lining everything up, which involved a lot of decision-making and mental labor, not to mention time, I then had to muster the energy to show up to the interviews to market the book.

This wasn't the smartest approach. By forcing all of that complexity and decision-making on myself, I was not only strapped for time, but my willpower was depleted. Despite having written the book about how willpower doesn't work, I was relying on willpower to launch that very book.

It didn't work.

I was exhausted before the book even came out, and thus, I didn't have the energy (or time) to continue marketing it after it launched. As a result, I didn't reach my goal of hitting bestseller lists and selling a specific amount of copies. I was doing too many Hows. I got caught up in the complexity and challenge of my goal, lost my focus, and as a result, lost my confidence. By doing everything myself, my results suffered. Hence, my *Freedom of Money* also suffered. You have to make investments to increase your freedom. You've got to step up and commit to doing things better and smarter, not solely working harder.

Thankfully, by the time I was preparing to launch my second book, *Personality Isn't Permanent,* I'd been learning Who Not How from Dan for quite some time. Rather than dealing with all of the e-mails and confusion involved in scheduling and media, I hired (or rather, had my assistant, Whitney, hire) someone solely for that task. All I needed to do was complete an Impact Filter stating exactly what I was looking for: someone who was organized and who was good at handling e-mail, setting appointments, managing multiple relationships, and making everything easy for me.

Connie came on board because when she read the Impact Filter, which clearly defined the vision and her role, she immediately identified with it. She knew she could do a brilliant job. The job was objective based and results focused: *Get me on 200 podcasts in 2020. Make the process incredibly easy for me, so that the only thing I have to think about is showing up.* Involved in completing that task was handling the key relationships, such as with the publicist at the publisher, and then doing all the pitching, scheduling, and back-and-forth with the various parties.

When it came time to start doing the podcasts, all I had to do was look at my calendar and show up. From February 2020 on, I'd regularly wake up and have five podcasts scheduled that day. I'd have an e-mail in my inbox with all the links to where the podcasts would be recorded.

I didn't have to think about anything.

No decision fatigue at all.

Connie had already made the hundreds of actions and decisions. The stage was set. By not having to deal with everything involved in setting the stage, I could just show up and perform. I didn't burn out my willpower through decision fatigue. Instead of navigating all the various relationships and scheduling hundreds of podcasts, I had a Who (Connie) do that for me.

It was an investment to hire Connie. It would have been easy to justify not spending the money to hire her. But had I not done so, I would have greatly limited my vision and what I was able to do. My goal would have shrunk, because without having a Who, I wouldn't have had the time to focus on simply performing the work I wanted to perform. By not hiring Connie, I would have reduced my *Freedom of Time,* which would have directly limited my *Freedom of Money.*

But with Connie, my goal actually grew, and I decided to shoot for being on 600 podcasts in a single year. The organization involved in making that possible would have been impossible for me. But with Connie's assistance, it was doable and stress-free. For her, it was a big challenge, but an exciting one. She loved the work and she loved watching me expand my vision and goal because of her contribution.

Because I was so excited by the growing size of the vision, and the ease with which it was being executed, I wanted to invest in Connie. I told her I'd give her a $10,000 bonus if we hit the new massive goal, and this got her excited because she was planning to go back to school, and the bonus would pay for most of her tuition. Once I made the single decision to hire a Who, *I never had to think about scheduling my podcasts again.*

Some people don't invest in Whos like Connie because they don't view them as an investment, *but as a cost.* They worry about the amount of money they'll have to pay their Who, rather than thinking about how that Who could elevate their vision and free up their time. The time I spend writing books and recording podcasts is worth at least 10X or even 100X the time I spent scheduling podcasts. If I'm scheduling podcasts, *I'm diminishing my potential for freedom of both time and money.* By having Connie support my vision, I have more time and more money. As a result, both Connie and I are more successful than either of us would have been without the relationship. Because I'm achieving more with her help, I'm making more. Because I'm making more, she's making more.

This is why Whos are an investment. More specifically, it is an investment in yourself. Every time you free yourself up by investing in a Who, you've just made a huge investment in yourself. You no longer have to deal with decision fatigue. Your vision can expand. Your income potential increases dramatically because you can focus on tasks that will make a huge impact.

The question is: *Are you going to add a Who?*

Do you want to free up your time and your mind?

What areas of your life and business most need a Who right now?

Remember the new question you must master: *"Who can help me achieve this goal?"*

Make the decision to add a Who and free yourself of the complexity of decision fatigue in that area. The research is very clear on this point: the more decisions you have to make, the lower the quality those decisions will become. You need to make fewer, but better, decisions. You need Whos to handle all of the involved decisions—whether that be scheduling or organizing—and set the stage *for you*. Don't set your own stage and then perform on top of that. Just show up and give the best show you can, whatever that looks like for you.

By better valuing and better maximizing your time, you will be enabled to radically improve your income. The quality of your work will improve. The clarity of your vision will increase, because you won't be so busy with all of the urgencies involved in the day-to-day. You'll have Whos to handle many if not most of your logistical decisions, giving you the Freedom of Time to make decisions that will ultimately create enormous amounts of money for you.

"You can have everything you love in life as long as you give up what you hate."

TIME IS MONEY

"Time is money."

—Benjamin Franklin

The quote above is probably the most famous quote about time by Benjamin Franklin, a man known for his productivity and amazing talents. In his 84 years, he became an influential politician and diplomat as well as an actor, musician, inventor, and satirist. The man knew the value of time.

The first freedom is *Freedom of Time*, which was covered extensively in Part 1. When you begin taking your own time more seriously, then the second freedom, *Freedom of Money*, starts to take care of itself.

Money avoids the person who doesn't value their time. Only those who improve their time, value it, and use it more effectively experience money freedom. Once you add Whos to handle your Hows, then your time will be best spent on those things that make the biggest impact.

Your vision will grow, which will demand that you make more money. As Charles Haanel explains in *The Master Key System*:

"Make the mental image. Make it clear, distinct, perfect; hold it firmly; the ways and means will develop; supply will follow the demand; you will be led to do the right thing at the right time and in the right way. Earnest Desire will bring about Confident Expectation, and this in turn must be reinforced by Firm Demand."

Motivationally, supply actually follows perceived demand. When you believe something must be done, you somehow find the ability to get it done. This is why deadlines are so powerful. When there is a demand or requirement, you find the motivation. Without that pressing demand, your needed motivational supply doesn't show up.

The famed historian, Will Durant, explained it this way: "The ability of the average man could be doubled if it were demanded, if the situation demanded." In psychology, this idea is called the *Pygmalion Effect*, and what it means is that as people, we are either rising or falling to the expectations of those around us. When the demands are high, we show up. When they are low, we settle.

David Bednar, the former president of Ricks College, told a story that further illustrates the notion that demand can facilitate the needed supply. In the story, a young man buys a new pickup truck and wants to test it. He drove up into the snowy mountains and ended up getting stuck in deep snow.

Frustrated and unsure what to do, he decided to get out, cut down a tree, and begin filling the pickup with wood. He expected that someone would drive by and could help him. No one came. Eventually, the back of his truck was entirely full of wood. He got back in the truck, said a prayer, and tried backing out. Surprisingly, with the weight of wood, the tires were able to get the needed traction to get out.

As Bednar explains, it was the load of wood that gave the traction needed to get unstuck and make progress. This principle applies to adding Whos to your goals and getting committed. You need to increase the demand on yourself to focus and succeed. You need an environment and situation forcing you to rise up to the level of your goals. In order to do that, you need to increase the demand on yourself and others to produce the desired result. Pressure can bust pipes or make a diamond. You need the pressure to succeed. You add that pressure by increasing your investment. This forces you to better use your time, which enables you to increase your income capacity or *Freedom of Money*.

Ours is a culture where people don't value their own time and instead want to win the lottery. They want money freedom without having earned time freedom. They want Freedom of Money with ease, which isn't how freedom is created. Freedom comes through purpose, investment, and teamwork. As is commonly the case with lottery winners uninterested in expanding themselves as people, they quickly lose all their money because they have no clue how to use their time. Having lots of money without valuing time leads to high levels of gluttony, self-destruction, and poor decision-making, until the money quickly evaporates.

Only those who value their time can become increasingly free in the realm of money.

"Don't twist yourself out of shape to be attractive to people you don't want to work with."

CHAPTER TAKEAWAYS

- You can't have money freedom until you achieve time freedom.

- By freeing up your time, you get the invaluable benefit of freeing up your mind.

- By freeing up your time, you can focus on higher impact activities—such as strategizing or creating—which will automatically increase your income.

- Improving how you spend your time automatically improves your ability to make money.

- Making the single decision to add a Who to a specific area of your life eliminates decision fatigue in that area.

- Eliminating decision fatigue from your life should be one of your primary goals if you want to be a high performer and increase your income.

CHAPTER 5

COMMIT TO SPECIFIC RESULTS

"Commitment is a statement of what 'is.' You can know what you're committed to by your results, not by what you say your commitments are. We are all committed. We are all producing results. The result is proof of a commitment."

—Jim Dethmer, Diana Chapman, and Kaley Klemp

In 2008, Nicole Wipp was a young attorney in Michigan where the financial recession hit particularly hard due to the auto industry crisis. Finding a job at a law firm was basically impossible for Nicole. Consequently, she decided to start her own firm.

For the next year and a half, Nicole was a solo show, working 80–100 hours per week. In addition to spending time in court, she was doing all the legal writing and research for her cases, responding to e-mails, and spending literally thousands of minutes on the phone with her clients. In her words, "I was grinding."

Nicole was also reaching a breaking point. It was becoming so bad that she was considering leaving the legal professional altogether. She was exhausted from doing everything herself. She was doing as much work as a three- or four-person team. She wasn't getting good rest. Her mind was always jacked up and wired, endlessly thinking of the never-ending pile of work to be done. She couldn't rest and recover. She couldn't be present with loved ones. On top of that, she was feeling a deep desire to have a child.

Something needed to change.

She wanted Freedom of Time to be a mom. She wanted Freedom of Money to have the life she knew she could have for herself and her family. While "grinding" and killing herself, she was not even making six figures, despite her talent and the insane hours she was working.

She decided not to leave the legal profession, but instead, to do it differently. She made the leap and hired her first employee, which ended up being a disaster because Nicole was not yet clear on her own vision, nor was she clear on what the new hire's specific role should be. She was scrambling and in reaction mode. But she learned many crucial lessons from this first hire and has since mastered Who Not How.

For instance, she learned that other people are capable enough to do most of what she was doing. Actually, she learned that others are *far* more capable of doing most of what she was doing. She also learned that her own recovery and time away from work was essential to her happiness and confidence, which directly impacted her performance and income.

Every time you invest in a vision, your commitment to that vision increases. By investing in that initial Who, as well as experiencing the painful lessons along the way, Nicole got committed. Psychologists call this *Escalation of Commitment*: Every time you invest yourself in something, you become more committed to it.

Her increasing commitment led her to intensely clarify her own vision for herself and her life. This included where she lived (she recently moved to Hawaii with her family), how much she worked, what areas of the projects she worked on, and how much money she made.

With this clarity of vision, she has been able to build a powerful team of committed Whos. She has several full-time staff members who have been trained to produce results. Nicole does no hand-holding, but she is there to support them when needed. She's extremely committed to her team and will go to hell and back for them if necessary.

Nicole wants her Whos to build the confidence in themselves that she already has in them. For instance, she once brought her paralegal with her to a business conference. During the conference, there was a group exercise in which each individual had to get up and introduce themselves to the group for two minutes. Nicole's paralegal was terrified and didn't want to do it. She tried to get out of it. But Nicole wouldn't let her off the hook.

Her paralegal reluctantly went through the exercise and, over the course of the conference, developed greater confidence and vision. She was having a transformational experience. With her leader's encouragement, she broke through emotional obstacles.

For Nicole, it's essential to commit to specific results and get your team on board. In order to do so, you can't let them off the hook. You've got to allow them to be challenged. They've got to face obstacles and break through them; otherwise, they'll never develop the confidence and commitment they need to fulfill your vision—and their own goals.

Nicole practices what psychologists would call *transformational leadership*.

Transformational Leadership Theory is the number one leadership theory in the world as of the writing of this book. Transformational leaders embody four characteristics:

1. **Individualized Consideration**: The degree to which, as the leader, you attend to each team member's needs, act as a mentor or coach to each member, and listen to concerns and needs. You give empathy and support, keep communication open, and place challenges before your team so they can grow. You give respect and celebrate the individual contribution that each person can make to the team.

2. **Intellectual Stimulation**: The degree to which, as the leader, you challenge people's assumptions, take risks, and solicit ideas from your team. You stimulate and encourage creativity in your team, and you nurture and help team members to think independently. You help them build confidence so they can make their own decisions and take their own risks. You take learning very seriously, placing high value on it, and you see unexpected situations as opportunities to learn. You allow your team members to ask you questions, and ultimately, make their own decisions about how to better execute their own tasks. You don't micromanage.

3. **Inspirational Motivation**: The degree to which, as the leader, you articulate a vision that is appealing and inspiring to your team. You challenge your team to increase their personal standards, while you communicate optimism about future goals, and provide meaning for the task at hand. Every member of your team needs a strong sense of purpose

in order to be motivated to act. Purpose and meaning provide the energy that drives the group forward. As the visionary and leader, your ability to powerfully and persuasively communicate the vision is essential. You must make the vision understandable, precise, powerful, and engaging so that your team will become increasingly willing to put more effort into completing their tasks. They'll exhibit encouragement and optimism about the future and believe in their abilities. They'll draw from your confidence and embody that within themselves.

4. **Idealized Influence:** As the leader, you act as a role model for high ethical behavior, you instill positive pride and create a culture among your team, and you gain respect and trust. People follow you because of who you are. You have high moral authority. People want to be with you, learn from you, help you, and be transformed through your vision.

To get the results she wanted, Nicole had to commit fully to her goals. Even more, she needed to get her Whos just as invested and committed, which she did by by *investing in them*, by challenging them, and by helping them have transformational experiences. She channeled her own confidence through them by never letting them off the hook.

She has built a very powerful, committed, and self-managing team. Even in the midst of the COVID-19 challenge, and with Nicole living in Hawaii while the rest of the team was in Michigan, all Nicole had to do was provide her team with the vision of what needed to be done.

Her team got straight to work, transitioning how they did things for their clients, most of whom were in their 70s and 80s, and thus considered "high risk" of contracting

COVID-19. They made the transition powerfully and without need for hand holding. Although they are facing a crisis, her team has the confidence and flexibility to handle difficult situations, because in the past, they weren't let off the hook in smaller matters.

"There are two kinds of suffering: long suffering and short suffering. The choice is yours."

SHOWING YOUR WHOS YOUR COMMITMENT AND CONFIDENCE

Dan Sullivan has this to say about risk and confidence: "Entrepreneurs have crossed 'the risk line' from the 'Time-and-Effort Economy' to the 'Results Economy.' For them, there's no guaranteed income, no one writing them a paycheck every two weeks.

They live by their ability to generate opportunity by creating value for their clientele. Sometimes, they—and you—will put in a lot of time and effort and get no result. Other times, they don't put in much time and effort and get a big result.

The focus for entrepreneurs always has to be on results or there's no revenue coming in. If you work for an entrepreneur, guess what! This is true for you too. Though you probably have a guaranteed income, it's important to understand that the business you work in exists inside the Results Economy, even if you're sheltered somewhat from seeing that.

I say this not to make you feel insecure, but to show you how to succeed in this environment: by maximizing your results while minimizing the time and effort it takes to get them."

If you want greater freedom in your life, *you'll need to focus on results.* You'll need to let Whos achieve the result for you. You'll need to give them the freedom to execute and create solutions in their own unique way. There is a great deal of science to back this up.

According to Self-Determination Theory, every human being has three basic psychological needs related to their work:

1. A sense of competence

2. Autonomy in how they do their work

3. Positive and meaningful relationships

Social environments that support these three needs create high levels of intrinsic motivation, psychological and physical wellness, and enhanced performance in all of their people. But how these needs are applied is a critical part of the formula.

Interestingly, though, research has found that teams who have high levels of autonomy but low goal clarity, as well as little performance feedback, actually perform worse than teams with low autonomy. However, when a team has 1) high autonomy, 2) high goal clarity, and also 3) gets regular feedback on their results, then their performance shoots through the roof.

Put simply, autonomy without clarity is ultimately a disaster. The Who will wander in circles freely but will not go in a meaningful direction.

This brings us to the primary issue with leadership: Lack of clarity of vision and inability to articulate that vision leaves Whos with no identity and no clear purpose. They become frustrated and lose their confidence. It's not because they lack the resources or capability, but because they have bad leadership.

Instead of providing radical clarity, giving profound trust and autonomy, and being committed to the results and flexible to the process, too many leaders obsessively micromanage the process of their Whos.

It is the role of the leader to determine the "what"—which is the desired outcome or goal—and to provide clarity, feedback, and direction when needed. *It is not the role of the leader to explain how the job is done.* The Who determines how they will best go about getting the job done. All they need is clarity about what specifically "done" looks like.

This is where the Impact Filter can be helpful. It helps all involved parties stay on track when confronted with other distractions. When building a house, there are many things you could add to the house that may improve it. But if those improvements distract from the details you specifically want for that house, then such "improvements" may actually kill the entire vision.

By having clear Success Criteria, meaning what has to be true when this project is finished, you can ensure your Who doesn't get lost. At the same time, you give them full autonomy in how they make that Success Criteria real.

Without clear boundaries, your Who will lose motivation. Boundaries and clarity create motivation. In order to be motivated, you need clarity and simplicity. Boundaries help clarify your path toward your desired aims. According to Expectancy Theory, one of the core motivation theories in psychology, motivation requires a clear and tangible outcome, as well as a path to getting that outcome. The constraints established by the Success Criteria are essential for the Who being motivated, because they clarify the Who's path but also provide complete autonomy in how they create the result.

"Always reward creators.
Never reward complainers."

CHAPTER TAKEAWAYS

- If you're truly committed to a result, you'll need to focus on Who, not How.

- Extreme commitment comes from clarity of vision and the autonomy to execute that vision in whatever way the Who sees fit.

- Transformational leaders invest in their Whos, challenge them, help them clearly see the vision, and ultimately, get their Whos just as committed and invested as they are.

- Without clarity of vision, autonomy is not effective.

- With clarity of vision, as well as consistent feedback on results, autonomy leads to high performance.

- Leaders should be committed to results, not to a particular process.

- Rather than micromanaging the process, leadership should provide freedom and autonomy as well as extreme clarity and high standards of excellence.

CHAPTER 6

IF YOU HAVE ENOUGH MONEY TO SOLVE A PROBLEM, YOU DON'T HAVE A PROBLEM

"Lessons are repeated until learned."
—Dr. Chérie Carter-Scott

Wesley ("Wes") Sierk is the lead strategist and former president of Risk Management Advisors, Inc., a company he sold for a handsome sum in the summer of 2019.

Wes is a brilliant guy, but like all of us, he's made some pretty big blunders in his life. One of these mistakes left him nearly dead and in a coma just two weeks after selling his company.

To explain how Wes almost died, we need to go back a few years. In August 2017, Wes was approached by someone who wanted to buy his company. Ecstatic, Wes engaged the potential buyer and began the negotiation process. Given that the potential buyer proactively reached out to him, Wes determined he didn't need to hire an investment banker, and that he could handle it all himself. But Wes had never sold a company before. In his own words, "I was doing something I knew nothing about."

While drowning himself in all the minutiae of selling the company, he neglected his role as CEO. This led to an extreme decline in productivity among his entire team. More than six months into this negotiation process, in March of 2018, both parties determined that they should split ways. The potential buyer no longer wanted the company, and Wes didn't get the result he wanted, after losing hundreds of thousands of dollars in attorney fees and productivity among his team.

Why didn't this work out for Wes?

The transaction seemed so easy and straightforward. Someone wanted what he had. Yet in the end, Wes didn't get what he wanted. And all for one single reason: *Wes focused on "How" instead of "Who."* Put bluntly, Wes didn't want to pay someone qualified to help him. He assumed he could do it himself, and even that he *should* do it himself.

Focusing on "How" creates problems.

After the failed transaction, Wes had to get back to work, picking up the pieces of a scattered business. From March 2018 to February 2019, Wes got his company back in order. Then he hired an investment banker to help him sell his company.

The first time he attempted to sell the business, Wes tried to negotiate eight times EBITA (earnings before interest, taxes, and amortization), which is a measure of company profitability used by investors to establish the perceived value of a company. However, the investment banker negotiated 10 times EBITA, and in a short time, was able to get five offers from interested buyers, one of which Wes ultimately agreed upon.

It took less than six months start to finish for the qualified Who to get the job done.

The investment banker's fee was approximately $500,000 to structure and secure the deal. But that fee pales in comparison to the time Wes saved by not doing it himself. Moreover, the investment banker sold the company for considerably more, *millions* more, than Wes had ignorantly tried to negotiate himself.

Not only did Wes save time, but he made tons of extra money by investing in a Who rather than trying to do all the Hows himself.

Back to Wes's mistake . . .

Two weeks after selling his company, Wes found that the air conditioner in his house had broken. He got a quote from an air-conditioning repair person and was pained by the proposed $7,900 fee for a new air conditioner.

Given that Wes was a former contractor, he decided he could save some money by rigging a big box fan and blowing it through the evaporator to ease the burden on the fan to cool down the house. He would then wait until winter—when people weren't buying air conditioners and thus they would be cheaper—to buy a new one. This would cost him a few hours up on his roof, but would save him anywhere from a couple hundred to a few thousand bucks.

It's important to note that Wes is a millionaire. He drives fancy cars, just sold a company, and is a well-educated and well-respected guy. He's also, in many respects, a frugal guy, raised in a small town in Virginia with much of his roots still deep within him. Some of his small-town thinking helped him become successful, and some has kept him stuck in small-mindedness.

On August 31, 2019, Wes climbed his ladder to put the box fan on his roof. It was swelteringly hot in the California sun. The next thing Wes knew, he was lying on his back on the concrete. He'd fallen from the roof, backward, and landed square on the back of his head, severely cracking his skull.

He rolled to the front door of his house and pounded. When his wife and sister-in-law came to the door, Wes was lying on the ground, nearly unconscious.

"What's wrong?" they asked, not sensing fully Wes's problematic situation. Initially, he just seemed exhausted, but within seconds, they realized the situation was far more stark.

"Nothing, I'm just hot. I'm hot and need to lie down," Wes replied.

He then rolled over and started vomiting, and that's when they saw the pool of blood. They immediately called 911 and rushed him to the hospital. At that point, he lost consciousness.

Wes ended up in the hospital for 11 days, two of which he spent in a coma. After leaving the hospital, which Wes doesn't remember, he was stuck in bed for two months. He needed a walker to use the bathroom. He couldn't talk and couldn't walk on his own and had to relearn basic skills.

During those two months of being bedridden, Wes was extremely depressed. He was mad at himself for having done something he shouldn't have been doing. He was terrified that his brain might never work the same way again. When his head smashed into the ground, his brain rattled back and forth so intensely that his face became swollen and bruised from the internal impact. He didn't know what his future held. His mind went to very dark places, and he felt incredibly alone.

There was a persistent thought consuming Wes's mind during those two months. It was actually a quote he'd heard from Dan: *"If you have enough money to solve a problem, then you don't have a problem."*

Ironically, Wes has known Dan personally for years. He'd heard that statement literally hundreds of times, both directly from Dan and from countless others quoting Dan.

"That thought kept spinning through my mind, because I did what I shouldn't have been doing," said Wes.

The neurosurgeon told Wes that over 50 percent of people who fall from their own height or above and land on their head die. Wes had faced death and the consequences of doing a "How" he didn't need to do, just weeks after having gone through the process of selling a company, which should have taught him that critical lesson.

After almost dying, the concept started to really sink in.

In December 2019, shortly after Wes recovered enough to get back to work, he did something bold. For the first time since 2003, when he and his wife bought their home, Wes hired someone to put up their Christmas lights. It sounds funny, but for Wes, it was a huge step. Almost dying led him to more fully value his time. He also realized the habits and limiting perspectives that had stopped him in the past.

He made a big, if simple, Who Not How decision.

He now realizes that if he has enough money to solve a problem, then he doesn't have a problem. He values his life, his time, his talents, and the contributions of other people enough to invest in Whos. Every investment—even a seemingly insignificant one of a few hundred dollars so someone else can put up his Christmas lights—is an investment in himself. He can now spend those five or six hours doing work that pays him 10X or more what he pays the Christmas light man to do. Or he spends that time with his loved ones or engaging in a hobby.

By early 2020, Wes had mostly recovered from his injury. He returned to the company he'd sold in a new role: marketing and growing the business. One of his goals was to master creating YouTube videos and Facebook advertising as marketing for his company.

After shooting his first video, he started learning how to edit. It was only after getting feedback from a colleague that it dawned on him that he actually owned a video production company, and that all he needed to do was send them the video clips and they'd edit them for him.

Wes is still learning. He's getting faster at going straight to Who rather than wasting his time and efforts on How. But Wes Sierk is not the only person who learned the costliness of "How." In fact, trying to do all the Hows is the normal way of doing things for most people. Our culture has brainwashed us into avoiding costs rather than making powerful investments in ourselves and our futures. As a result, we willingly do all sorts of "busy" or ineffective work outside our expertise and passion, falsely believing that "working hard" or engaging in such tasks is worth it.

Although having a great work ethic is something to strive for, you've got to be careful. You're either in the "Time and Effort Economy" or the "Results Economy." Far too often, people wear their hard work as a badge of honor. But in reality, they are engaging in Hows that could easily be handled by a Who to more effectively produce the desired result.

"No one ever lost any advantage by being humble, interested, and useful."

AVOID THE "COST" MIND-SET

"Only once you give yourself permission to stop trying to do it all, to stop saying yes to everyone, can you make your highest contribution toward the things that really matter."

—Greg McKeown

Carl Castledine was born near London in 1969. His father was a poor coal miner. By all accounts, Carl's father was an amazing and loving man who wanted the best for his son. However, given their financial situation, Carl's father taught him some deeply limiting and destructive beliefs about money.

These beliefs daunted Carl for many years.

Carl was pressured to go into management because, from his father's point of view, that would be the surest path to "success." Management was viewed as risk-free and would allow Carl to have much more than his parents had.

Carl succumbed to the parental pressure and pursued a career in management. Even though he really wanted to be a musician and artist, he worked hard at being a manager. But it became incredibly obvious to himself and to everyone around him that he hated his life. He didn't feel alive and wasn't excited about his future.

His job brought him to a project in the leisure and tourism industry. Carl loved what he saw: smiling faces and happy people enjoying vacations and resorts. He decided he wanted to stay in the industry, but he needed to spread his wings. He felt incredibly limited in his role. Rather than working in management as he had done, he decided to start his own company. He wanted more freedom to create vision and help people have incredible vacation experiences.

In 2013, he created his company, Away Resorts, and like most entrepreneurs, Carl worked insane hours. By sheer grit and willpower, he was able to build up a decent clientele. But his business's growth was far less than it could have been. Carl knew his company needed more of an online presence and a much better website. On top of the ridiculous hours he was already working, he began staying up all night learning to code for several months.

He literally spent hundreds of hours as the CEO of a company, learning to code and build websites. His company was being neglected. His sleep was being taxed. His energy was draining and his patience running thin. At a breaking point, with bags of exhaustion under his eyes, he decided to ask a web developer how much it would cost to build a website. To his surprise, the man said he'd happily do it for £1,200.

Carl's face went white.

In his own words, he felt like donkey ears grew out of his head like in the cartoon film *Pinocchio*. He said he felt like a "jackass." The low amount of the fee shocked him, given the amount of time he'd invested as well as the value of his time as CEO. Yet like with so many others, this lesson seems to take a few repetitions to finally sink in. You've got to really learn the opportunity cost of How. By doing everything yourself, you miss out on unfathomable growth that comes by investing in Whos and utilizing your time and efforts on higher impact activities.

For years, Carl managed the sales team of his company. By all accounts, he did a good job. But in 2017, he decided to hire a sales manager so he could focus on other aspects of the company. Within a year of hiring this sales manager, the company's profits went up 25 percent, netting an additional £2.5 million during that first year. The sales manager's salary was £120,000.

"Had I hired that guy seven years ago, we would have likely made another fourteen to fifteen million pounds," Carl stated directly.

That was the last straw for Carl.

He decided to go all in on Who Not How.

He's not being conservative about it at all now that he sees the power of it. He is no longer willing to burn time like he did before. His time matters too much to him. His standards have elevated. He's committed to results now. He's committed to freedom. He's not going to blow his time and future on stuff that other people would gladly do for him.

Carl was trained to think in terms of cost, rather than investment. He now realizes the power of investing in himself and his future. Every time he invests in a Who, such as paying someone £1,200 for a website, he saves himself dozens or hundreds of hours that he can spend doing something more valuable and profitable. That time, if used focusing on the right things, could add millions of dollars to the bottom line. By hiring the sales manager for £120,000, Carl not only freed up time, but the company's revenue grew by several million in the first year.

This is the power of thinking in terms of investment. It wasn't a cost to add that sales manager. It was actually costing Carl and the company to not have him.

Joe Polish, the founder of Genius Network, often tells his entrepreneurs that Genius Network is a school that pays you to attend. To be a part of his school requires a $25,000 investment. But those who make that investment, become part of the network, and learn from the group can easily turn that $25,000 into several hundred thousand or millions.

But people often don't make such investments themselves. They don't see how such investments could easily lead to outcomes that are 10X bigger or more. I myself am a part of Genius Network, which is how I was able to connect with Dan Sullivan, Tucker Max, and Reid Tracy.

Without having invested in that network, this book wouldn't even exist. I wouldn't have had the *Freedom of*

Relationship (to be discussed in Part 3) to access such brilliant collaborators. The only way I was able to create the transformational relationships available in Genius Network, or any other network, is by seeing it as an investment, not a cost.

I was quite surprised, actually, that during my first Genius Network meeting, many of the other entrepreneurs in the room were asking how they could ensure they get the "return on investment" for their $25,000. To me, this was incredibly small-minded. It wasn't about getting the $25,000 back. That's a cost mind-set. Rather, it's about multiplying that $25,000 investment by 10X or 100X. And the only way to do that is by engaging in transformational relationships.

When you're investment-minded, you're not short-term in your thinking. You consider the bigger picture, and you look at how you can help the right people, without coming across as transactional.

If you're cost-minded, then by nature, *you're transactional* and short-term focused. You'll see Whos as a cost, which means you'll never be able to create the brilliant collaborations that are possible. Whos, when selected properly to fit within your vision, are never a cost. **Whos are an investment.**

If you're investment-minded, then you will be transformational in your relationships, including the relationship you have with yourself. You'll be long-term focused, having an increasingly growing vision of your future. You'll see that by investing in Whos, your future can dramatically grow.

You'll also be transformational, not transactional, in all decisions you make. For example, when you decide to take the day off work to spend time with your family, you won't see that as a cost. You'll focus on the investment you're making in your loved ones.

By shifting your focus from cost to investment, you stop worrying about what you're giving up and instead, realize that by making powerful decisions you can make enormous gains.

"You can survive without a community,
but you can't thrive without one."

CHAPTER TAKEAWAYS

- Focusing on How will greatly limit your ability to make money.

- Believing that doing all of the Hows yourself is noble is a limiting belief. *It's not noble.*

- When you focus on How, it's often based on a scarcity mind-set and cost avoidance.

- Trying to avoid costs by engaging in Hows will cost you and your future huge in the long run.

- By seeing Whos as an investment, rather than a cost, you can quickly 10X or more your income and revenue.

- By seeing Whos as an investment, rather than a cost, you can create transformational relationships, in which all parties give more than they take, rather than transactional ones.

- By seeing yourself as an investment, rather than a cost, you can expand your Freedom of Time, Money, Relationship, and Purpose.

PART 3

FREEDOM OF RELATIONSHIP

CHAPTER 7

HOW TO BE A GOOD WHO FOR OTHERS

"You're either in communication or trying to escape."
—Joe Polish

Joe Polish is the founder of the high-level marketing mastermind groups, Genius Network and GeniusX, as well as the nonprofit Genius Recovery Foundation. Both *Forbes* and *Inc.* magazines have called Joe "the most connected man in business."

In writing this book, I personally interviewed dozens of entrepreneurs about how they applied Who Not How. Not surprisingly, in many of those interviews, Joe's name would inevitably come up. He's an extremely important Who for many people. Dan calls Joe a "node," which by definition, is a point at which lines or pathways intersect or branch, a central or connecting point.

Without Joe Polish, this book would not exist (as I said, it was through Genius Network that I met Dan Sullivan, Tucker Max, and Reid Tracy). Not only is Joe unique in how he approaches, develops, and maintains relationships for himself, but also he has a singular approach to helping others develop relationships as well.

Joe doesn't believe he has the answers to everyone's questions. Instead, he believes that with the right "genius network," any problem in the world can be solved. Thus, rather than being the point man for everyone's problems, Joe has created a network of world-class entrepreneurs, experts, marketers, doctors, influencers, and innovators. When people enter Joe's world, they not only get Joe, but they get the extension of Joe, which is his living and breathing network of geniuses. That's why he calls it Genius Network.

But there's a catch.

In order to successfully navigate Joe's network, and really, in order to be successful with high-level people in general, you've got to understand how genuine connection and transformational relationships work. There is quite the vetting process that one must go through in order to enter Joe's network. And once you're in, if you want to get the most out of it, you've got to approach relationships in almost the exact opposite way that is typical in society.

Once you understand this higher level, strategic, and conscious way of approaching relationships, *you'll be able to connect with basically anyone*. You'll be able to create 10X, 100X, or bigger collaborations—meaning you'll create relationships that, over time, produce positively skewed returns. You'll be able to expand and grow as a person in dramatic and often unexpected ways.

To help you more fully implement Who Not How, the remainder of this chapter details Joe Polish's philosophy and strategies on relationships. You will learn the mind-sets needed to make transformational relationships the standard for all of your relationships, whether it be with your spouse, friends, your clients, or your team. The goal is for you to refine your own filter, so that you experience true *Freedom of Relationship*, which means you have not only increasing access to whatever Whos you need to achieve your goals, but you also have deeper and higher quality relationships overall.

Your ability to succeed is based on the quality of the people in your life. As you increase your Time and Money Freedoms, you'll have greater access to Whos that not only help you achieve your goals but also give you a deeper sense of meaning and purpose in your life. Freedom of Purpose, then, is measured by your ability to connect to and develop relationships with particular people. The more freedom you have, the more access you have. But not just access. . . you'll also have the ability and reason to connect and develop partnerships with chosen Whos.

"Treat your employees as an investment,
not a cost."

ARE YOU DRAWN TO THEM?

"What you seek is seeking you."

—Rumi

Joe sees relationships like he sees clothing. If an outfit doesn't fit right, if it's too tight or too baggy, or if it's not functional, *then the relationship doesn't make sense.*

First and foremost, when it comes to connecting with someone, you should *want* to be connected with them. It shouldn't be a chore. There shouldn't be any desire to avoid contact or escape from them. There should be no need for posturing or posing. But rather, you should feel completely free to be yourself, and ultimately, who you aspire to be.

"How do I feel when I'm with this person?"

That's a key distinction for Joe when thinking about relationships. If he doesn't feel drawn to the person, if he doesn't feel amazing around them, if he's not inspired or connected, and if it's not easy, then the relationship is a no-go, regardless of how credentialed or "successful" the person is.

"I don't want to work on a relationship. I just want a relationship that works," Dan told Joe years ago, in discussing his relationship with Babs. Joe held on to that concept and it has served him well.

When finding Whos, don't settle. Create transformational relationships with people you're drawn to and excited to be around. Find Whos that fit.

"Always test your ideas on check-writers."

YOU MUST CREATE VALUE FIRST

"Try not to become a man of success, but a man of value. Look around at how people want to get more out of life than they put in. A man of value will give more than he receives."
—Albert Einstein

Rather than asking, *"What's in it for me?"* which is the common question, Joe asks, *"What's in it for them?"*

Asking, *"What's in it for me?"* is a terrible way to get access to people. It is impossible to create transformational relationships with this selfish "taker" mind-set. The "what's in it for me" mind-set is transactional and small-minded and will only attract similarly transactional people.

Avoid these types of people like the plague.

They are takers, not givers.

They are parasites who will only be around until they've sucked whatever "value" they can from a group or relationship, then they will move on to their next prey.

Before Joe connects with someone, he does his homework. He wants to really know who the person is, what their context is, what they value, what they care about, and what they're trying to accomplish. Only then can he approach the relationship in a relevant and mindful way for the sole purpose of providing incredible value to *them*.

For instance, Joe met business magnate Richard Branson for the first time at a dinner that was organized to raise money for Richard's foundation, Virgin Unite. Joe made a $15,000 donation to Richard's charity. In exchange, Joe was invited to have dinner with Richard and a small group of other donors.

At the dinner, while some people were trying to extract as much value as they could from Richard, Joe sought to add value to Richard. Joe shared an idea with him that involved distributing a video that would educate people about Virgin Unite and its cause in hopes of increasing donations.

Joe explained to Richard how utilizing education-based marketing could take Virgin Unite's message to the whole world. And if people understood more about the organization, they would be more likely to support it via their time, efforts, and contributions.

After hearing the idea, Richard asked Joe if he could put it in writing and send it to his personal e-mail address, which he gave to Joe.

"I believe I'm the only one who got Richard's e-mail that evening," said Joe.

Now, years later, Richard has spoken at several of Joe's events, and Joe has traveled to Richard's private island (Necker Island) multiple times. Indeed, Joe has spent a lot of time with Richard. All of this happened without Joe even asking for Richard's time. Instead, Joe was useful and some-one Richard easily wanted to be around.

Joe's altruism didn't stop there, though. After he gave Richard that idea, he then asked if he could interview Jean Oelwang, the person running Virgin Unite, so that Joe could promote the interview to his contacts, subscribers, and fans.

Through this interview with Jean, many more peo-ple were educated about Virgin Unite and inspired to get involved. In fact, at one of Richard's "Rock the Kasbah" gala fund-raisers, 92 people came as a result of Joe and his Genius Network and each person made a $2,500 contribution to Vir-gin Unite. During the auction held that night, many of Joe's Whos bought items to support Virgin Unite. Joe has become Richard's single largest fund-raiser, having raised millions of dollars for the charity.

The moral to the story: ***Don't reach out to someone unless you have something meaningful to offer them.*** That "something" needs to be real and relevant, not just a com-pliment or flattery. True and real value. And if you want the relationship to continue, you must continue creating value.

When creating relationships with Whos, ask yourself, "What's in it for them?" When creating a vision, be sure that vision aligns with your Whos' objectives and clearly helps them achieve what they personally want.

"You have to work less to make more money."

CONTINUE NURTURING THE RELATIONSHIP

"Successful givers are every bit as ambitious as takers and matchers. They simply have a different way of pursuing their goals. . . . If you insist on a quid pro quo every time you help others, you will have a much narrower network. . . . Givers succeed in a way that creates a ripple effect, enhancing the success of people around them."

—Adam Grant

Joe loves this quote: "Be nice to the people on your way up, because you'll meet them on the way down."

When you first start a relationship, it's easy to be a giver. Usually, that's because you know what you can get out of the relationship. In the beginning of your career, you get paid for what you do. But if you become highly successful and influential, then over time, you'll get paid for who you are. Once you get what you want, or once you've gotten a little bit of fame, there is a tendency to believe your own publicity. You need to be careful of this happening.

Unless you're committed to the "What's in it for them?" mind-set, and continue to nurture your relationships, then you'll burn a lot of bridges along the way.

This isn't a useful approach to success.

Many people desire to be liked and to have status more than they desire to simply do good work. When status is your focus, then once you've obtained the status you want, you'll rest on your laurels. You'll ride the fumes of your former successes, and stop being as useful or concerned for others.

If you don't yet know how to connect with people in this more conscious and reciprocal manner, a great way to learn is simply by volunteering. Learn to serve other people without any expectation for reward. Learn to devote yourself to a cause, and to other people's goals, even if you get no fanfare. Examples of service could be volunteering to take inbound calls for a suicide hotline, supporting a political campaign (Dan has done this many times), serving at a homeless shelter or soup kitchen, acting as a missionary for a particular faith or cause, etc.

If you're useful, and continue being generous, the world will be very good to you. You'll have all the opportunity in the world you need because you'll have Freedom of Relationship. Never stop providing value to your Whos, especially the Whos that have been in your life for a long time.

"Surround yourself with people who remind you more of the future than the past."

THE SUPREME IMPORTANCE OF GRATITUDE

"Self-made is an illusion. There are many people who played divine roles in you having the life that you have today. Be sure to let them know how grateful you are. Example: the person who introduced you to the person who introduced you to your spouse or business partner or client. Go back that far."

—Michael Fishman

"The deepest craving of human nature is the need to be appreciated."

—William James

Being grateful goes a long way. Of course, you need to be genuinely grateful but also consistently grateful. When you're grateful, people will want to help you more. They'll want to work with you and be around you. People have an innate need to be appreciated and valued. When you generously and sincerely thank them in specific ways for the big and small things they do for you, you'll be changed as well. You'll become a kinder, humbler, and happier person. You'll also attract increasing Whos into your life, because gratitude attracts and creates abundance.

Psychological research has found that people who practice gratitude consistently report a host of benefits:

Physical

- Stronger immune systems
- Less bothered by aches and pains
- Lower blood pressure
- Exercise more and take better care of their health
- Sleep longer and feel more refreshed upon waking

Psychological

- Higher levels of positive emotions
- More alert, alive, and awake
- More joy and pleasure
- More optimism and happiness

Social

- More helpful, generous, and compassionate
- More forgiving
- More outgoing
- Feel less lonely and isolated

CHAPTER TAKEAWAYS

- Never enter a relationship without having first created value in that relationship.

- Never stop creating value and nurturing your relationships.

- Always ask "What's in it for them?" rather than "What's in it for me?"

- Know what the other person cares about.

- Get to know them, their context, and their goals. Give relevant value. Don't waste their time. Do your homework.

- If you want to develop transformational relationships, then approach relationships in a transformational, rather than transactional, way.

- Bring a result to the table. Make the pie bigger for everyone involved. Don't come with big promises of future results. Bring immediate results. Don't promise what you can't deliver.

- Be a generous giver who is truly committed to service and growth, not status.

- Be nice to the people you meet on the way up because they are the same people you meet on the way down.

- Be grateful in large and small ways to the people in your life and you'll attract incredible abundance.

CHAPTER 8

HOW TO AVOID THE WRONG WHOS, EVEN HIGHLY ATTRACTIVE ONES

"Intelligence is the ability to make finer distinctions."
—Robert Kiyosaki

Kate Gremillion is a 29-year-old entrepreneur and strategist living in Raleigh, North Carolina. She's creating a successful business that affords her a great income and complete control over her schedule, which she enjoys, as she recently got married. Although her life is amazing now, two years ago she was in the hospital, close to death.

Like many other entrepreneurs, Kate was doing way too much. Kate was stuck in the trap of "more." She believed doing more activities, having more clients, and having more features on platforms like *Forbes* would increase her revenue and success. Even though she was a great success on paper, and was accumulating more and more "credentials" and lines on her resume, she was working too many hours and literally killing herself to keep up with the identity she was conveying to her clients, of someone who had it all together. Then she was diagnosed with endometriosis. It took her two months to get to back to baseline, and even to this day, she still manages it daily by reducing her stress. Getting Whos and "outsourcing" became essential after the diagnosis because stress manifests the symptoms.

Looking back on her former self, Kate recognizes that it was actually ego that kept her burning the candle at both ends. She genuinely believed she was the only person who could successfully do most of what was required. Kate was doing way too much, and it didn't end well. But Kate is a really great learner, and she used that experience to change everything about what she was doing. She decided to get out of the partnership she was in and totally wipe the slate clean on her life and get back to her core principles:

What did she actually want?

Who did she want to be?

What was she no longer willing to do?

What was going to be different about how she approached things in the future?

Having time gives you the space to seek clarity. Kate wasn't giving herself time before, but being sick and thinking about her future allowed her to conceptualize who she wanted to be—her future self. She imagined and designed her circumstances, how she worked, who she worked with, and what her life would look like.

Kate created a new consulting company focused on helping entrepreneurs create systems that maximize their income and minimize busy work. Rather than running herself ragged, she built this company around the ideal lifestyle she wanted to have. She had firmer boundaries and clearer priorities. She wasn't going to throw herself under the bus again. She was going to make her business work for her rather than the other way around.

Kate built a small team, and together they've created much firmer ground rules about the types of clients and people they want to work with. In the past, Kate would willingly, although frustratingly, engage in phone calls and e-mail correspondence with people who, it turned out, were clearly not a good fit. Many times, random people who hadn't done their homework would reach out to her for basic business advice, information that was clearly available through her podcasts and blogs.

Kate has now created multiple buffers to ensure that only the right people get on her schedule. She's trained her assistant to filter through the e-mails and inquiries that come in. They've created an approval process for people to get access to Kate. If people don't meet the specs of what Kate is looking for, they are graciously rejected. Consequently, Kate's time is now spent far more powerfully. The conversations she has are more relevant and in-line with how she wants to serve her particular audience. There is little time wasted.

Kate's former self was willing to tolerate conversations and clients that didn't fit. Now she only engages with the types of Whos she wants to work with—people who can truly utilize what she has to offer. She wants to be an amazing Who, a "hero" to those she chooses to take on as clients. It's not about what she can get out of the relationship. It has to be the right Who so that both parties can have the optimal experience. Hence, Kate's Freedom of Relationship has greatly expanded, which generates greater income and time.

"If you work on something important for twenty years, it will transform everything around you."

YOU LEARN MORE ABOUT A LEADER BY WHAT THEY SAY "NO" TO THAN ANYTHING ELSE

"When deciding whether to do something, if you feel anything less than 'Wow! That would be amazing! Absolutely! Hell yeah!'—then say 'no.'"

—Derek Sivers

Chad Willardson is the author of *Stress-Free Money,* and the founder and president of Pacific Capital, a premier wealth management firm in Southern California. Chad gets several referrals for potential clients every week. However, on a particular morning in 2019, Chad received an e-mail from a client saying they had a huge referral—someone who just sold his business, netting him $100 million on top of the significant wealth he already had.

Obviously, this was exciting news for Chad. For most financial advisors, any time they can add a few million dollars per year to their investment base in new clients is great. Adding a single $100 million client is massive.

Chad started doing all sorts of homework on the guy, his business, and his family background. And as it so happened, they were both at the same event later that week. To Chad's surprise, this man approached Chad and said, "Hey, you're the guy I've been looking for. We've got some big things to talk about."

He told Chad he had met with many investment banking teams and private wealth groups at the big Wall Street firms but felt drawn to meet with a boutique and private advisory team, where he could get more personalized advice and individual attention. They set up a Skype call for the following week.

Before the Skype call, Chad made sure he was incredibly well prepared. He and his team were very excited about the prospect of working with this new client and his family. However, within the first five minutes of the call, Chad had some reservations, and his instincts were telling him this would be a very difficult client. The man was abrasive, condescending, and extremely high maintenance. He spent several minutes telling him about all the firms he had already talked to, and all the perks and discounts they had already promised him. He gave Chad a list of demands that would be required if they were to work together.

He was telling Chad how Pacific Capital and the team would have to adapt to doing things differently for him, and how he would be in contact three to five times a week to let them know what to do. Essentially, this would be like going to the doctor as a patient and telling the doctor what they should prescribe for you and how frequently.

This man didn't want to get a Who and let that incredible Who do the How.

He wanted to tell the Who what the Who should do.

Throughout the call, Chad kept his cool. He answered all the man's questions. When the man asked to meet some of the team members, those team members came into Chad's office and had a brief introduction via Skype to share their roles and describe how they serve the clients. He replied to each team member, telling them what he'd expect them to do differently for him, and was condescending in each conversation.

It was clear he was going to be a very demanding and challenging client.

After the call ended, Chad sent this man an e-mail recapping the phone call and highlighting the main points of their conversation. The e-mail also laid out Pacific Capital's services for high-net-worth clients, and an explanation for why they would be a great professional addition to his existing team to help him meet his personal and financial goals.

Shortly thereafter, Chad received a long e-mail response from the man filled with several more demands and expectations than were covered in the Skype call. Chad felt these expectations were not only unreasonable, but unproductive. That night Chad also started getting multiple text messages from the man further expounding on what he expected from every person on staff.

The next morning, which was a Friday, Chad and the team did their daily morning huddle. As a team, they discussed what they thought about this potential new client. Several team members, including the client service directors, said they felt very disrespected on the phone call. They expressed concern that he would be an extremely difficult client, but that they understood, given the size of his portfolio, how much this big client would mean for the firm and said that they would figure out how to deal with his demands.

Over the weekend, Chad spent quite a bit of time reflecting on this opportunity. He was going back and forth in his mind, asking himself several questions about how they could help the new client.

How can we make it work with the fewest problems possible?

Maybe he seems demanding now, but won't that get better over time?

Are we going to have to bend our core principles too much to accommodate him?

Is it worth it?

Chad was not 100 percent clear as to what he should do. It would be such a massive client and possibly open other doors for the firm. He also wondered about the impact on his team's morale and confidence if he, in essence, said that they should bite their tongue and deal with whatever this man wants, because "look at all the revenue he brings into the firm."

That didn't resonate with Chad at all. He ultimately concluded that if someone was condescending and disruptive to his team, and if they had unreasonable demands, then no amount of money would be worth it. He decided it was a no-go.

Throughout that weekend, Chad continued to receive numerous texts and e-mails from the prospective client, who repeatedly stated his demands and expectations. Chad replied to the man that they should set up a midweek follow-up call next week.

Once they got on the phone, the man quickly began reiterating his needs. Chad then said, "I really appreciate even being considered to work with you and your family. However, after talking with my team, we feel you would be better served working with someone else."

"What are you talking about?" the man replied, surprised. Quickly, his shock turned to anger. This man was not used to being rejected. He was much more used to everyone catering to his demands and wants.

"We appreciate this opportunity, we really do," Chad said. "But we don't feel it's a great fit. There are certainly companies out there that would want to do what you're looking for, and we wish you the best of success going forward."

The phone call ended awkwardly, but once he hung up, Chad felt empowered.

By saying "no" to this ultra-high-net-worth client, Chad gained enormous trust and confidence from his team. It certainly would have been easier to reject the situation if the potential client had only $2 million. They were all relieved that Chad had chosen to prioritize doing what was right over was what was lucrative. A potential burden had been lifted from the office. Chad's decision injected happiness and clarity into the team. This was a great experience for

Chad as a leader. He'd taken a big step in establishing Freedom of Relationship.

Chad was able to make this choice because, in the past, he'd seen the impact of working with clients who were not the right fit. With such clients, there was always a strained relationship and dissatisfaction. Their values and vision didn't align, and nothing could be done about it. They hired Chad's team but didn't want to take their advice or appreciate their service. In those wrong-fit cases, the relationship would eventually end, with one party suggesting they part ways.

At this point, Chad is completely unwilling to work with people who aren't the right clients for Pacific Capital. He ends up rejecting (politely) far more referrals than he accepts. "It would be a disservice to my team and a disservice to the new client if we agreed to work with people who aren't a great fit," Chad told me.

As an individual and as the head of a company, Chad has both Freedom of Time and Freedom of Money. As a result, he is quite clear on what he wants for himself, and his company and can be choosy about who he works with and who he spends his time with.

When Chad has meetings with right-fit prospective clients, he's not desperate. He's serious about being the best Who for those he works with. If he can't be the best Who for them, he won't work with them. As he tells prospective clients:

"Look, there's absolutely no pressure for you to work with us. This is a two-way interview, and we are both evaluating if it's a great fit. If you choose a different advisory firm, we will be absolutely fine. We only want to work together if we are excited and 100 percent on the same page for goals and expectations. Being aligned and upfront with each other from day one is crucial to a successful long-term relationship. And in the end, that's what it's all about."

"We remain young to the degree that our ambitions are greater than our memories."

ALWAYS BE THE BUYER

"Never allow someone to be your priority while allowing yourself to be their option."

—attributed to Mark Twain

According to research done by Harvard psychologist Dr. Daniel Gilbert, a person's personality—their preferences and attitudes—change over time. Take, for example, yourself.

Are you the same person you were 10 years ago?

Do you see the world exactly how you did 10 years ago? Or even five years ago?

Are you focused on the same goals?

Do you have the same priorities?

Do you want exactly the same things?

How do you spend your time now versus how you used to spend your time?

Do you tolerate the same things?

Dr. Gilbert has found that, consistently, people can see changes—often big changes—in themselves when looking over the past 10 years. Kate and Chad are just two examples of people who have adjusted in how they do things. In this way, the past should serve as important information and learning, allowing you to approach life and your future differently.

Kate and Chad are no longer willing tolerate the things they once did. They're increasingly committed to being the best Who they can be for the right Whos for them.

Shannon Waller, an entrepreneurial coach and strategist, made the same discovery, but with a slight distinction. Six years ago, Shannon finally hired her own executive assistant. By freeing herself up from much of what she had been doing, Shannon quickly realized that what she formerly saw as critical was actually not. Activities she once believed could *only be done by her*, she now realized could easily be handed off to a Who. The result is that Shannon immediately had far more time to focus on bigger-impact projects, which were far more in line with her passions and goals.

Chad was able to reject the high-net-worth client in part because of his recent experiences with overly demanding clients. Furthermore, Chad was able to reject a seemingly great opportunity because that opportunity would limit, not benefit, his future self. He wanted to hold on to his values. He wanted to become a powerful leader, someone who could say no to potentially negative experiences. Because Chad was clear on his future, he could reject seemingly incredible opportunities in the present.

Now it's your turn. Take some time to reflect on the following questions:

How have you changed over the past five years, when it comes to the types of people you surround yourself with?

What things do you no longer tolerate?

How have you become a better Who for the people in your life?

Dan has a saying for this: "Always be the buyer." What he means is that, in every situation you're in, you should be the one who is buying, not selling. The buyer can reject the seller, not the other way around.

Chad is a buyer. He chooses his clients. Just because someone wants to work with him doesn't mean they can.

That's *Freedom of Relationship.*

You can become the buyer in all aspects of your life. You do this by rejecting anything that isn't in line with your vision. Being the buyer takes courage, but over time, it will become the only way you engage in relationships. You will become incredibly picky about your relationships because you're incredibly clear about who your future self is, your vision, and your priorities.

When you begin saying "no" to people, obligations, and situations you don't feel fully aligned with in your gut, then and only then will you be able to expand your confidence and purpose. Instead, you will engage only in high-value relationships, where both Whos—yourself and the other person—are totally aligned and can enhance each other in powerful ways.

"Personal confidence comes from making progress toward goals that are far bigger than your present capabilities."

CHAPTER TAKEAWAYS

- In order to have Freedom of Relationship, you can no longer engage with people that don't align with your vision.

- You can build buffers and systems to ensure you no longer directly work with people who aren't relevant.

- As you say no to people and opportunities that don't align with the vision of your future self, your confidence will increase. Your team will also become more confident in you as a leader.

- Your current self no longer tolerates situations and people that your former self once tolerated.

- Your future self will not tolerate nor engage with situations or people that you currently tolerate.

- As you make courageous decisions based on the future you want to create, you can make bolder leaps into your freedom and success.

CHAPTER 9

HOW TO CREATE EFFECTIVE COLLABORATIONS

"No matter how brilliant your mind or strategy, if you're playing a solo game, you'll always lose out to a team."
—Reid Hoffman

Wherever you see incredible work happening, there is collaboration, even if it doesn't seem so. Take golf, for example. Golf seems like an individual sport. But when you get down to the nitty gritty, it's actually not.

In a Professional Golf Association (PGA) match, each golfer is supposed to "go it alone." However, each golfer *can* have their caddy with them. A caddy carries the golfer's bag and clubs, but also gives insightful advice and moral support, acting as helper, teacher, strategist, and psychologist. Although their importance doesn't seem crucial, a good caddy will make or break you at the highest level of golf.

The relationship between Tiger Woods and his caddy, Steve Williams, is the ultimate example. Williams was Tiger's caddy from 1999 to 2011 and did more than carry Tiger's bags and provide encouragement. He also taunted and jeered Tiger to get his blood boiling, to spark Tiger's competitive edge if he was lagging.

Sometimes, Williams would even intentionally misinform Tiger if he thought it would improve Tiger's game.

At the 2000 PGA Championship, in the fourth round and on the fairway of the 17th hole, Tiger was behind by one shot. He needed a birdy to tie the leader. Williams calculated 95 yards to the flag, but he purposefully told Tiger 90 yards. Williams knew Tiger's game and his patterns just as much, if not more so than Tiger. In an interview with *Golf* magazine, Williams said:

"Tiger's distance control had become a problem. . . . He had trouble hitting three balls the same distance three times in a row with the same club. So, I would adjust yardages and not tell him. If he had 95 yards, I might tell him 85 yards, depending on how he was swinging."

At that 17th hole, and based on Williams's advice, Tiger hit the ball two feet from the hole and ended up winning the three-hole playoff. Williams had been giving Tiger incorrect yardages for five years, which also happened to be during Tiger's most successful run.

For the remainder of this chapter, I'll break down key aspects of how to effectively collaborate during specific projects.

"Support is attracted to purpose."

BE OPEN TO AND RELY ON OTHER PEOPLE'S SUGGESTIONS

"Without contraries is no progression."

—William Blake

Tiger relied heavily on Williams's ideas, perspectives, and strategies. Sometimes Tiger would push back or disagree. But often, Williams would change how Tiger thought about a particular situation or strategy.

The first key to engaging in high-quality teamwork is to not think you know exactly what you're doing. You've got to be open to other people's ideas. You've got to realize that other people's ideas, solutions, or strategies can be *far superior to your own*. And that's a good thing!

In the classic book, *Think and Grow Rich*, Napoleon Hill describes how lawyers for a Chicago newspaper attempted to prove that Henry Ford was ignorant by asking him loads of strange questions. "Who was Benedict Arnold?" and "How many soldiers did the British send over to America to put down the Rebellion of 1776?"

Finally, Ford became tired of the absurd questioning, and in reply to a particularly offensive question, he leaned over, pointed his finger at the lawyer who had asked the question, and said:

"If I should really want to answer the foolish question you have just asked, or any of the other questions you have been asking me, let me remind you that I have a row of electric push-buttons on my desk, and by pushing the right button, I can summon to my aid men who can answer any question I desire to ask concerning the business to which I am devoting most of my efforts."

Henry Ford was wildly successful and innovative *because* he knew how ignorant he was. Rather than having to know everything himself, or being an expert in all things, he was incredibly good at Who Not How. He welcomed and sought other people's perspectives. He got incredible people to design, engineer, manufacture, sell, and distribute his cars.

You are only one person. As brilliant as you are, your current views are very limited at best. By combining your perspectives and skills with those of others, your thinking and results can improve dramatically.

"Technology is a team member that keeps getting smarter and faster."

FAST FEEDBACK LOOPS WITH ENCOURAGEMENT (APPLY THE 80 PERCENT RULE)

"A painting is never finished—it simply stops in interesting places."

—Paul Gardner

"Eighty percent is already getting results while a hundred percent is still thinking about it."

—Dan Sullivan

On March 29, 1967, John Lennon met Paul McCartney at his house in London to work on a song for Ringo Starr to sing that they'd started the day before, hoping to record it later that night.

Hunter Davies, a journalist for the *Sunday Times*, was with them and took notes about how John and Paul worked together. Davies wrote:

"John started playing his guitar and Paul started banging on his piano. For a couple of hours they both banged away. Each seemed to be in a trance until the other came up with something good, then he would pluck it out of a mass of noises and try it himself."

That evening the whole group went around the corner to the EMI recording studios to finish the song.

They all spent several hours in the studio with Paul playing piano, George Harrison on electric guitar, Ringo on drums, and John on a cowbell. It took 10 takes, but they finally created a track they were happy with.

Ringo received lots of support and encouragement from his friends. As Geoff Emerick, who was one of the sound engineers at the session, recounted in his memoir, *Here, There and Everywhere: My Life Recording the Music of the Beatles:*

"All three of his compatriots gathered around him, inches behind the microphone, silently conducting and cheering him on as he gamely tackled his vocal duties. It was a touching show of unity among the four Beatles."

However, there was one final catch. The climax of the song called for very high singing notes. Ringo was terrified and later stated that it took a lot of support to hit those notes, particularly from Paul.

After several attempts, he successfully scaled the vocal heights. Everyone cheered and the session was over. And the name of that song? "With a Little Help from My Friends." You often need encouragement to be courageous. That's what teamwork is all about.

This story is a powerful illustration of creativity, teamwork, and innovation. It's a back-and-forth process. Rather than sitting by yourself, trying to perfect the idea without feedback, it's far more effective to throw your ideas out there fast, get feedback from your team, and then adjust as you go.

The faster you get at throwing out incomplete work, the faster it will transform into something great. Dan calls this the 80 percent rule. You can get to 80 percent of a project very quickly, such as writing a rough draft. However, going from 80 percent to 90 percent is exponentially more work than going from 0 to 80 percent. Going from 90 to 100 percent is a mountain. You just need to do what you can do as the Who, and then quickly pass it off to the next Who.

The longer you try to perfect your idea before feedback, the slower the transformation process. Get your Whos involved. Stop trying to do it all yourself. The sooner you get teamwork involved, the faster and better your work will be. Also, with encouragement, you'll work through challenges instead of procrastinating as you would naturally.

Finally, get used to "publishing" or sending out imperfect work. Nothing is ever truly "finished," only "done." Done is better than perfect.

"What people want to buy most is their own future."

RADICALLY OPEN AND FAST COMMUNICATION (AND ASKING FOR HELP)

"Emotion, which is suffering, ceases to be suffering as soon as we form a clear and precise picture of it."
—Viktor Frankl quoting Spinoza's Ethics in
Man's Search for Meaning

"Anything that's human is mentionable, and anything that is mentionable can be more manageable. When we can talk about our feelings, they become less overwhelming, less upsetting, and less scary. The people we trust with that important talk can help us know that we are not alone."
—Mr. Rogers

At some point or another, on the way to achieving your goals, you'll get stuck. The "Hows" you're doing might be too challenging, or life will happen. The sooner you can be open and honest with those around you about how you're feeling, the sooner things can start moving forward.

The worst thing you can do, when you're struggling or stuck, is keep it to yourself. By being vulnerable and honest about your feelings, you'll immediately be less overwhelmed. You'll be able to see your emotions differently once they are communicated openly. But also, you'll begin making progress toward the result, because rather than avoiding painful emotions, you'll be committed to moving forward.

Dan has said, "All progress starts by telling the truth." I learned this lesson while writing this book. I had a particularly short timeline and, for a period of a few weeks, was a bit overwhelmed by the task at hand. But I didn't tell anyone I was stuck or overwhelmed. I just procrastinated, got stressed out, and ultimately, got super sick.

With the deadline pressing, I was nowhere near where I needed to be. I was also sick as a dog and incapable of working. It got to the point where I needed to share my plight. I opened up to Tucker about the situation. "Why didn't you tell me sooner?" he asked. I didn't have a good reason, except that I was scared to ask for help, scared to admit I didn't have all the answers.

Unfortunately, my lack of open communication put the team's goals in jeopardy. Deadlines are real things. And in order to get this book published when we wanted to, we needed to create results fast. The first thing that needed fixing was my emotional state. Tucker helped me clarify why I was so emotionally stuck. To be honest, I was worried about making this book something Dan would like. I'd never coauthored a book before, and working with Dan was a dream come true. Rather than being myself, and writing in the way I know how to, I got all caught up and worried about what Dan would think of the book. This got in the way of my creativity. I also wondered how much autonomy I really had in making this book the way *I* wanted it to be.

Tucker was able to help me realize that the best thing I could do was create the book I wanted to create. Dan wanted me, as the Who, to fully own the How. This was my book. This was my How. I was the Who. I needed to take full ownership. No one else could write the book I was going to write. That's why I was the Who. I just needed that permission, which Tucker helped me get. That permission gave me the confidence to write the book I wanted to write, and to not worry so much what others thought about it.

Additionally, I was able to get clarity from Tucker about how to logistically structure the book. In order for one to be motivated, they need a clear path forward. Often, you need a Who to help you formulate that path, so you can get yourself moving again. A few conversations with Tucker, someone who knows books much better than I do, helped me create a structure I loved. Once that structure was in place, and I had the permission to be the Who, then I could move forward.

I only wish I had had the courage to communicate my needs sooner. I would have saved myself and the team a lot of stress and heartache. But as Dan says, "Always make your learning greater than your experience." Hopefully, I learn from this experience so I don't have to needlessly repeat it in the past.

Whatever your role, responsibility, or challenge, the sooner you communicate your needs the better. Not only will you clear your emotions, but you'll get the clarity needed to be motivated. You'll also realize something incredibly essential and important: that the people in your life and on your team truly do love and care about you. It's always humbling to see just how much those around you do care and want you to succeed. It is during your moments of humility and vulnerability when you discover this, and it actually increases your commitment to the team. By seeing how much you're cared for, you become more committed to your team. You feel an increased desire to do your absolute best work so you can be a hero to those with whom you work.

"Ambition and success need no justification."

GENUINELY SEEK TO BE A HERO TO YOUR TEAM (YOUR "WHOS")

"For success, like happiness, cannot be pursued; it must ensue, and it only does so as the unintended side effect of one's personal dedication to a cause greater than oneself or as the by-product of one's surrender to a person other than oneself."

—Viktor Frankl

"Who do you want to be a hero to?"

—Dan Sullivan

If you genuinely want to be a hero to your collaborators, you'll show up for them. You'll do your best work. You'll produce the needed results.

If you're transactional, and just trying to move the needle for yourself, then you may produce in the short term. But you won't break through some of the huge challenges that come with doing big projects. You won't make it through the messiness that often is transformational growth.

I'm always blown away by how much Dan wants to be a hero to his Whos. I've experienced this myself. He's willing to help me in incredible ways because he wants to be a hero to me. This makes me, as his Who, want to be more of a hero to him.

Everyone on your team should want to be a hero to you, and to one another. Likewise, as a leader, you should want nothing more than to be a hero for your team. That can and should become *your purpose*, to be a hero. You will do your best work and ensure you produce results because you genuinely care about the vision and genuinely want to be a hero to your Whos.

"Getting results doesn't take much time at all.
It's not getting the results that takes
up all the time."

CHAPTER TAKEAWAYS

- Wherever you see brilliant work happening, collaboration is happening.
- You don't have all the answers. It's wise to consider yourself ignorant on most things, and to seek other people's perspectives and solutions.
- Apply the 80 percent rule to move projects forward by not over-obsessing about your part of the project. Get feedback fast!
- Be radically open and honest in your communication. Ask for help when you need it.
- Seek to be a hero to those you work with, and you'll do your best work for them.

PART 4

FREEDOM OF PURPOSE

CHAPTER 10

STOP COMPETING AND START COLLABORATING

"A creative man is motivated by the desire to achieve, not by the desire to beat others."

—Ayn Rand

For the past 20 years, Karen Nance, an attorney in San Francisco, has wanted to write a biography about her grandmother, Ethel Ray Nance—an important civil rights activist who gained national recognition in 1923 for breaking the secretarial color barrier in the Minnesota State Legislature.

This desire led to Karen making a Who Not How shift, which ultimately expanded her *Freedom of Purpose*. *Freedom of Purpose* is the sense of vision and purpose you have for your life. Your sense of purpose expands as you see deep meaning and value in what you're doing. Said Viktor Frankl, "Life is never made unbearable by circumstances, but only by lack of meaning and purpose." The more deep and powerful your sense of purpose, the more meaningful your life will be. But also, the more committed you'll be to do whatever is required to live that purpose.

As it related to her own sense of purpose, Karen had felt a divine sense of duty to get her grandmother's story out into the world. In fact, a few years back, she finally started writing the biography. However, she was quickly dismayed by the process of bringing this project to light. Writing a biography is *a lot of work!*

Despite her best efforts, Karen's progress was lackluster and slow. Sometimes she could focus on the biography, but more often than not, the project sat on the back burner and wasn't anywhere close to being done. It's not that she was incapable of writing it or without purpose, but she's a busy attorney with a full-time job and is engaged in other important activities that really matter to her.

But the biography remained on her mind, and she couldn't escape thinking about it on a daily basis, all the while feeling a sense of urgency and frustration at her lack of progress as well as the realistic distance to completion and publication. "It will get done at some point . . . even if that's five to ten years from now," she thought.

However, 12 months ago, Karen received an e-mail that heightened her urgency to complete the biography. Dr. Ethelene Whitmire, a history professor at the University of Wisconsin-Madison, was writing a biography about Karen's grandmother and was hoping to get additional information.

In the e-mail, Dr. Whitmire explained that she was an expert on black feminist history in America and had already published a biography about Regina Anderson Andrews, an important black feminist figure who was the cousin of Ethel Ray Nance. Dr. Whitmire had no clue Karen was also writing a biography. In the e-mail, Dr. Whitmire explained that she was already 100 pages into the writing of her biography. Karen's initial reaction was to not share any information with Dr. Whitmire.

Why would she help this woman?

They were in competition with each other . . .

Karen already had written 200 scattered pages. She was going to need to get busy in order to beat Dr. Whitmire to publication.

But given that Karen was incredibly busy and booked up with work demands, her increased urgency turned into increased anxiety and stress. With every passing day, she knew Dr. Whitmire was making progress on her biography. They were in a footrace to the finish.

Karen did take some solace in the idea that she had insider information that Dr. Whitmire would not be able to access, since Karen wasn't going to share it with Dr. Whitmire. The best thing Karen could do was ensure Dr. Whitmire was limited in the information she had, and to get her own biography written as quickly as possible, despite the fact that she was too busy to write and had never actually written a biography before.

I met Karen in January 2020 and she told me this story. She had come to me for coaching and support in helping achieve her 2020 goals. Karen is an incredibly ambitious and inspiring woman, who is dedicated to human rights in America. In the midst of her many goals was her grand-mother's biography, something she really wanted to get done. Something she felt needed to be done in 2020, given the situation with Dr. Whitmire, even as she was working on her other high priority of positioning herself as an authority on human rights.

I knew it would be impossible for her to complete this biography in a meaningful way in less than a year. She'd been working on it for several years and was nowhere near being done. And her other work demands were only increas-ing. She simply didn't have the time or the capability. This isn't to say she isn't competent. But writing a biography is not something you do flippantly. Especially if you're trying to honor your grandmother and create something of lasting value and impact.

There was really only one answer: Karen needed to stop competing and start collaborating. She needed to drop the scarcity mind-set and increase her abundance and vision. She needed to stop working in isolation, putting all the pressure and Hows on herself, and instead, she needed to get an amazingly qualified Who to do a much better job than she could dream of doing herself. And as it just so happened, there was a brilliant history professor and biographer who was already engaged in Karen's goal . . . they just weren't on the same page yet.

"What would happen if you just coauthored the book with her?" I asked Karen. The question seemed to stun her into silence. I went on to explain:

"Wouldn't the book be better if you collaborated and joined forces? Also, she's a seasoned biographer. This is what she does for a living. She probably has access to a publisher, media, and other forms of outreach you don't have access to. You wouldn't have to do any more writing but could pass off everything you've done to her and she'd take care of it. The book will become unfathomably better than you are currently imagining. Even more, you both would be the messengers, allowing your grandmother's story to go further and impact more lives."

It was so easy and obvious that Karen felt immediately *relieved*. Not only would this solution free her from the rut she had been in on the project but also working with Dr. Whitmire would be an incredible blessing! How lucky was Karen that a professional biographer, who was also a history teacher and expert on the very subject Karen cared so deeply about, happened to be interested in writing this biography on her somewhat obscure grandmother? Karen was starting to feel this was radically fortuitous. This biography was going to become a lot bigger and more important than she had initially imagined.

That's what happens when other Whos get involved, the project becomes more important and impactful—this is an example of *expansion* or Freedom of Purpose through Who Not How. By adding Whos to what you're doing, with greater capabilities and perspectives where you're weak, the initial vision you had will automatically expand. Your goal becomes far better than anything you could conjure up on your own.

I challenged Karen to immediately e-mail Dr. Whitmire with the idea of coauthoring the book. Karen sent the e-mail and got a fast response. Dr. Whitmire was completely ecstatic to coauthor the biography.

Karen now had a Who.

She no longer needed to procrastinate or feel guilty. She no longer needed to engage in competition and needless anxiety. The completion of the project was now inevitable. Moreover, the project would be far better, be done far faster, and would reach countless more lives because it was now a collaboration.

Karen could now focus all of her attention on her other pressing goals. She is growing an important nonprofit that focuses on human rights, and that role perfectly matches her skills and passions.

Yes, the biography gave her purpose, and yes, she could have painstakingly figured out how to do it. But at great cost. Had she continued on her own, she would have neglected the role she is currently in and the important work she's so passionate about.

Now, there is no compromise. Her grandmother's biography is being done by someone who is an expert at writing biographies. And Karen is able to focus her attention where she wants it. Both projects get to make progress and move forward at the same time because Karen is not the only Who involved.

"Entrepreneurs base their lives on results.
It's not about time or effort."

STOP BEING ISOLATED IN YOUR GOALS

"Too much self-centered attitude, you see, brings, you see, isolation. Result: loneliness, fear, anger. The extreme self-centered attitude is the source of suffering."

—Dalai Lama

In elementary school, you were taught that getting help from others is "cheating." You were not taught to enlist the help and capabilities of your peers. Yet in the world of business and life, collaboration is the name of the game. Getting help from others not only enables you to create success in your life but also gives you a deep sense of meaning and belonging.

When you focus on "How," you quickly become isolated in your goals. Focusing on How comes from the faulty reasoning that you are 100 percent responsible for getting the job done. This may lead to a good work ethic, but ultimately, it's not smart. There is no reward for doing lots of tasks and working yourself to death in mediocre fashion. Results are what count.

Being isolated and alone in your goals does damage to your perspective, warping you into a cynical person with limiting views of yourself and other people. You undervalue the contribution of other people and also underestimate what you could be and what you could accomplish.

Your vision shrinks and becomes focused on what you solely can do, and you stop relating well with others. You see people dogmatically and inflexibly, including yourself. You never grow into a leader or decision-maker. You don't experience the joys and transformation of teamwork and growing success. You limit your freedom.

The antidote to being isolated in your goals is asking: "Who can help me accomplish this?"

The fact of the matter is this: You don't have to feel guilty for not doing everything yourself. You're not less of a person for getting help. You're not cheating.

Even more, there are hordes of brilliant and talented people out there who'd love to help you with your goals and objectives (and get your help with theirs).

Rather than spending your day feeling guilty and frustrated, and limited in what you can do, you could feel incredibly grateful that you have amazing people who not only *will* help you but *want* to help you!

"The only way to be remembered fondly is to increase others' capabilities."

COMPETITION COMES FROM A SCARCITY MIND-SET AND EGO

"Competition is for losers."

—Peter Thiel

Humans have survived and thrived because of their ability to communicate and collaborate with others. Even still, most people have not developed their abilities to create a vision, make decisions, be leaders, or build teams.

As a culture over the past 100 years, particularly in America, there has been a huge emphasis and push toward both competition and "How."

The traditional education system supported the industrial model, wherein students were not taught to collaborate, lead, and do teamwork, but instead were taught to generalize in a bunch of Hows and take meaningless and abstract tests. This system fosters a sense of competition, wherein a person's self-worth is based on how they individually do on a test or assignment against other individuals.

It is no wonder, then, that the primary business cultures in corporate America are highly individualistic and competitive, rather than collaborative.

According to research by Dr. David Logan, a business professor at the University of Southern California, most business cultures are what he calls, "Stage 3 Culture," which is epitomized by internal competition wherein each person is out for themselves, willing to backstab, gossip, or do whatever it takes to get the position above their colleagues.

Much rarer are "Stage 4 Cultures," which emphasize teamwork and collaboration—focusing on the quality and characteristics of the group rather than the individual. Stage 4 Cultures are far more productive and successful than Stage 3 Cultures in business and sports.

We already talked about Phil Jackson, the legendary basketball coach who oversaw all six championships in the Michael Jordan era of the Chicago Bulls and all five championships of the Kobe Bryant and Shaquille O'Neal–led Los Angeles Lakers. He said that his Bulls were primarily a Stage 4 team. It's the reason they made history and changed the basketball world forever.

There were phases where the Lakers were Stage 4, and during those phases they won championships. But often, his Lakers were a Stage 3 team, competing with each other for who got the ball or who would take the final shot.

Kobe and Shaq often struggled to work together, each wanting to be the lead man. The competition between them ultimately drove Shaq to another team. And although they won three championships together in three years straight—the years they operated as a Stage 4 team—it is speculated that had they been able to remain a team, Kobe and Shaq had the potential to win several more championships together, and become the most dominant duo of all time.

Henry David Thoreau famously stated in *Walden* that "the mass of men lead lives of quiet desperation." We believe that the main reason people do this is because they've been taught to think individualistically, rather than collaboratively.

Given the exponential rise in technology, information, and globalization, the world is shifting out of the mediocre and limiting the "How" model. The public education system is under scrutiny for its teaching methods and principles. More and more people are seeking work that is collaborative, flexible, and meaningful. Those who are good at creating connections with mentors, teachers, and partners have the potential to create incredible wealth and freedom.

Even more, given the speed at which technology is advancing, "Hows" that were once done by specialized individuals are getting outsourced and delegated to machines. No matter how skillful you think you are, five years from now, those skills may not be valued. But your ability to connect with people, learn, and collaborate is becoming increasingly valuable in today's society.

We are no longer in the "How" world with its limitations. Instead, we are in a world where "Whos"—including technology—allow you faster and bigger results and more freedom than ever before. The age of competition and "How" is dying. Consequently, we are far more enabled to generate *Freedom of Purpose*. We have more options. It's easier to find a need to fill, create a team to support you, and to make tangible impacts on people throughout the world.

"The only way you can make your present better is by making your future better."

CHAPTER TAKEAWAYS

- Focusing on "How" makes you rigid and non-collaborative in your thinking.

- Focusing on "How" stresses you out, because you're already busy and can't juggle it all.

- Focusing on "How" leads you to being isolated in your goals, and ultimately slows your progress.

- Being isolated in your goals diminishes your dreams.

- Competition stunts creative innovation and limits your future.

- Collaboration immediately expands your *Freedom of Purpose* and vision, because what you can do with others is exponentially more than what you can do by yourself.

- Collaboration allows you to focus on what you want to focus on and not feel guilty about getting help.

- Collaboration transforms the initial intent of the project into something surprisingly better and more impactful than you would have planned on your own. By expanding your vision, your Freedom of Purpose also expands.

CHAPTER 11

WHOS EXPAND YOUR VISION AND PURPOSE

"If you organize your life around your passion, you can turn your passion into your story and then turn your story into something bigger—something that matters."

—Blake Mycoskie

In January 2015, during the first year of my doctorate in organizational psychology, Lauren and I became the foster parents of three siblings. We ended up spending three years in court trying to adopt these three children.

The foster system, and particularly, our case worker, did not want us to adopt our three kids. She was openly and aggressively against us having these kids. She was prejudiced against us and didn't like us because we were openly seeking to adopt our three children, which from her perspective, was not our right nor our role. On one occasion, she broke the law by taking the kids from our care and illegally giving them to their grandmother, who had failed a home study and was not eligible to have the kids.

A few hours later, she reluctantly called us, rudely asking if we still wanted the kids back. We told her that of course we did.

"Then meet us at the Walmart parking lot in an hour," she told us.

We followed her instructions and got our children back that day, but it was clear that we'd need to take immediate action to prevent anything like this from happening again. In the midst of our terrible situation, and without surety we'd be able to adopt the kids we loved, we felt grateful to learn of an adoption attorney in the state of South Carolina who not only knew the law better than anyone else, but who also was actively fighting to change the laws in South Carolina to create greater freedoms and opportunities for foster parents, which at the time were incredibly limited.

The attorney's name is Dale Dove, and it was amazing to see how the case changed once Dale got involved.

Dale had several similar cases to ours that were under way at the state courts, and eventually, he was able to clarify the laws in South Carolina that needed refinement, particularly around the rights of foster parents being enabled to proactively seek adoption of children who didn't have healthy familial options. Thanks to his incredible work and knowledge of the law, we were able to adopt our three children. It was a total miracle, and something we could have never done ourselves.

We needed a Who in order to adopt our children, not a How.

Our children have transformed and expanded our purpose, and Dale Dove, through his inspired and compassionate work, made it possible for us to adopt our kids.

FIND WHOS THAT EXPAND YOUR VISION AND PURPOSE

"Alone we can do so little; together we can do so much."
—Helen Keller

In the 20th century, two British authors, J. R. R. Tolkien and C. S. Lewis, dominated the world of fictional fantasy. Tolkien's *The Lord of the Rings* and Lewis's *Chronicles of Narnia* books have sold well over 300 million copies combined, and continue to leave a footprint on modern culture. But what most people don't realize is that without their friendship, none of these books would have been written.

Without C. S. Lewis's encouragement, it's doubtful that J. R. R. Tolkien would have ever written *The Lord of the Rings*. Without Tolkien's prodding, Lewis may have never converted back to Christianity, which deeply influenced Lewis's books.

Without proper context, it's easy to assume that Tolkien was a lone genius, and that *The Lord of the Rings* books were always somewhere buried within him, their publication inevitable. But that is fanciful and ignorant thinking. Tolkien's thoughts were heavily influenced by Lewis's, and without that meshing of ideas and the confidence that ensued, Tolkien wouldn't have—he *couldn't* have—written those books.

A keystone concept in psychology is known as the *fundamental attribution error* (also known as correspondence bias or over-attribution effect), which is the tendency for people to overemphasize dispositional or personality-based explanations for how a person acts while underemphasizing situational explanations.

In Western culture especially, where we focus so much on the individual, there is a strong cognitive bias to assume that a person's actions depend on what "kind" of person they are, rather than on the social and environmental forces that influence the person.

A year after Tolkien began teaching at Merton College at Oxford University, he met Lewis, a fellow professor, at a faculty meeting in 1926. They didn't hit it off initially. Lewis described Tolkien in his journal as "a smooth, pale fluent little chap—no harm in him: only needs a smack or so." But the pair soon connected over a shared interest in Norse mythology.

Over the next few years, Tolkien, Lewis, and a few others would meet informally in a private back room (called the Rabbit Room) of the Eagle and Child pub on the Oxford campus. The literary group, which called themselves, "The Inklings," would meet to discuss and workshop one another's endeavors, and it was during these group meetings that Tolkien and Lewis found inspiration.

On December 6, 1929, Tolkien asked Lewis if he would look at his poem, *The Lay of Leithian*, which consisted of more than 4,200 verses and told the story of the mortal man Beren, who escaped to the world of elves and fell in love with the immortal elf maiden Lúthien. Tolkien had been privately working on this poem for four years. Given the unique nature of his work, Tolkien was apprehensive to share. But Lewis agreed to read it.

A day later, Lewis wrote to Tolkien, expressing his enthusiasm: "I can honestly say that it is ages since I have had an evening of such delight; and the personal interest of reading a friend's work had very little to do with it."

After his praise of the story, Lewis said that detailed criticisms, as well as complaints about individual lines would soon follow. Shortly thereafter, Tolkien received a deeply thoughtful and comprehensive list of feedback, from the overarching themes to suggestions for replacements of individual words. Lewis suggested specific revisions and even rewrote sections of the poem.

Tolkien appreciated Lewis's perspectives, and heavily revised his poem to include many of Lewis's suggestions.

It was incredibly risky, from Tolkien's perspective, to share his work with Lewis, to expose himself and his art so deeply. But after providing feedback on Tolkien's work, Lewis took the similar risk of sharing his own poetry with Tolkien, who likewise provided substantial and unsparing critique and feedback.

Decades later, in 1965, after having written his epic trilogy and experiencing wide success, Tolkien wrote a letter to Dick Plotz, speaking of Lewis:

"He was for long my only audience. Only from him did I ever get the idea that my 'stuff' could be more than a private hobby. But for his interest and unceasing eagerness for more I should never have brought The L. of the R. to a conclusion."

He would have never had the courage or confidence to complete *The Lord of the Rings* without Lewis. Even more, without Lewis's feedback and encouragement, Tolkien would have been unable to create such a masterful work. He needed a Who. But likewise, Lewis needed a Who as well.

While Lewis was encouraging Tolkien to continue mapping out his universe, he himself was undergoing a crisis of faith. On a fall evening in 1931, Lewis took a walk with Tolkien and another fellow Inkling, Hugo Dyson, and they prodded Lewis back to his faith. By dawn Lewis had decided to return to Christianity, his rededication to which completely revolutionized Lewis's imagination and creativity, fueling his most important work and legacy.

Lewis needed a Who.

Tolkien needed a Who.

Without each other, their incredibly important work would not have become what it did. Indeed, their work may have never been known.

More than the impact of their work, which obviously has been immense, it was the encouragement and support they received from each other that ultimately transformed and expanded their individual purposes in life.

Tolkien would have never taken his work seriously. He would have never undergone the arduous challenge of completing, let alone publishing, *The Lord of the Rings*. Lewis would have never seen for himself the purpose of striving to convert so many to his faith. It was by having a Who that these men were able to expand their purpose to reach and influence many people.

The same is true for you. Your identity is not fixed, but rather based upon your current experiences. Your identity and purpose will expand as you have experiences of encouragement and support through the right Whos.

Moreover, by getting certain Whos involved in your current goals and vision, that vision will expand and grow dramatically. Take, for example, the story of Lee Richter and her husband, Gary, who own Holistic Veterinary Care, a hospital for animals in California.

Gary is an award-winning veterinarian, and their company has revenues of more than $100 million per year. One of the core reasons for their success is the way Lee approaches relationships.

A few years back, she met Chrissy, an amazingly talented woman who ran leadership expert Richard Rossi's huge events, which usually have 12,000 or more attendees. Gary was speaking at the event, and Lee immediately took notice of Chrissy.

Despite the fact that some of the world's largest influencers and celebrities were speaking at the event, Chrissy treated

Lee and Gary like they were important and special. Quickly, Lee and Chrissy developed a friendship and stayed in touch.

A few years later, Chrissy was applying to a few positions and called Lee seeking advice. Lee made a quick judgment call, based on two things. First off, she believed in Chrissy's talent. Even though there were no open positions for Chrissy at the time, Lee would create one because she wanted that level of talent on her team. Second, she knew that Chrissy had a deep passion and love for animals, and animals were what her and Gary's business was all about.

Lee made Chrissy an offer on the spot. "Don't apply to jobs in the insurance space. You're not passionate about that," Lee told her. "Come work for us. I know you love animals. You can do work that matters to you."

"When you see talent like that," Lee told me, "you get them on board and then find out what to do with them. All you need to do for people like Chrissy is set the stage and let them go."

Within a year, Chrissy was made the chief marketing officer of all nine of their companies. Aside from applying her marketing talents, Chrissy has actually transformed everything they do at Holistic Veterinary Care. Lee and Gary are both committed to caring for animals. But since adding Chrissy to the team, Gary's passion and sense of purpose have increased dramatically. Chrissy's enthusiasm is spreading, giving deeper meaning and significance to everything they're doing.

In addition, Chrissy comes from a totally different perspective than Gary and Lee. Chrissy is a pet owner and has been for years. She knows the perspective of Holistic Veterinary Care's clients better than anyone, because she is one of their clients. She knows how pet owners feel. She knows what they think about, worry about, and care about. Consequently, she's constantly pitching brilliant ideas and suggestions that the team wouldn't have come up with.

There's something else that's incredibly important when you get a Who on your team who enhances the passions and purpose for everyone involved—they give you confidence to try new and bigger things. In Lee's case, she's always wanted to do a "moonshot" in the animal healthcare space.

The first moonshot was announced to the US Congress in May 1961 when President John F. Kennedy declared his intention to put a man on the moon by the end of the decade. By 1969, that goal was achieved when Neil Armstrong became the first man to walk on the moon. Inspired by that monumental achievement, Google has repurposed the term "moonshot" to refer to its pursuit of lofty goals that, if successful, would change the world, just as Neil Armstrong did more than 50 years ago. Since 2010, Astro Teller, director of the semi-secret facility Google X and self-described "Captain of Moonshots," has overseen the development of bold projects like self-driving cars, Google Glass, aerial wind turbines, and Project Loon, which aims to bring Internet access to remote regions using helium balloons.

In February 2016, Teller laid out the principles of the "moonshot" philosophy. A moonshot, he said, should first be about solving "a huge problem in the world that affects many millions of people." Second, it should not settle for half-baked measures. It has to provide a "radical solution" that can do away with the problem for good. Teller's last criteria is the reasonable expectation that technology can actually solve the problem. Moonshots should be as much about pragmatism as they are about dreaming.

Lee's friend Steven Krein is the founder of StartUp Health, a conglomerate of more than 130 companies. Krein is currently pursuing nine "moonshots" in the healthcare space, seeking to innovate and improve the lives of millions of people in various ways from curing cancer and other diseases to ending addiction.

Once Lee had Chrissy on her team and saw the impact she was making throughout all of their companies, Lee started thinking about the moonshot. She'd wanted to do something major in the animal care space but didn't have the confidence. Until she had a Who, that is.

She decided to call Steve and ask him about collaborating on a moonshot focused on healthcare for animals. Steve was game, and now Lee and Gary are attempting bigger projects than they ever dreamed of before. None of this would have been possible had Lee not invested in Whos that she knew were worth it, even if in the beginning, she wasn't sure what role they would play.

"When going into new situations, you have
to know what is nonnegotiable."

WHOSE HERO DO YOU WANT TO BE?

"I think of a hero as someone who understands the degree of responsibility that comes with his freedom."
—Bob Dylan

JANCOA Janitorial Services, Inc., was founded in 1972 as a small family business, but over the past six years it has nearly doubled in size all without a sales team and without advertising. JANCOA has more than 650 full-time employees and cleans more than 18 million square feet nightly throughout Cincinnati, Ohio.

JANCOA owns nearly 80 percent of the Cincinnati market for corporate janitorial services, and their competition is completely mystified by how JANCOA does it. According to Mary Miller, the CEO and co-owner of JANCOA, the primary reason JANCOA is so successful is because they acknowledge the humanity of their employees and use JANCOA as a platform to help them live their dreams.

Given the type of work JANCOA performs, many of their employee's lack education and many are immigrants from other countries. Often, janitors don't get the respect they deserve in corporate settings.

A key shift happened for JANCOA when Mary and her husband, Tony, who founded JANCOA, really got to *know* their employees. They asked all their employees what their major struggles and challenges were in terms of being successful at their job. They found that the primary obstacle was reliable transportation to work. Many of their employees don't have their own vehicles. This insight led Mary and Tony to team with local transportation services in Cincinnati to provide free transportation to employees who needed it. As a result, employees were less stressed about their commute, were able to get to work on time on a consistent basis, and had better work/life balance because they spent less time commuting to and from work.

The quality of the lives of their employees is very important to Mary and Tony. They were committed to removing obstacles that were preventing their employees from being successful. But they don't just want to remove obstacles; their primary motivation is to dramatically improve the quality of their employee's lives in all dimensions. Therefore, they don't just knock down obstacles, but they strive to help their employees develop a sense of mission and purpose in life. For instance, they have events where they give special recognition to outstanding employees. They provide financial as well as other gifts. They also provide many opportunities for continuing education and personal development. They encourage their employees to set huge ambitions far beyond JANCOA and to use JANCOA as the means to get there.

In an industry that averages a 400–500 percent annual turnover rate, JANCOA boasts an 85 percent annual turnover rate. The reason for that significant difference is that their employees love being there. There is a culture of caring at the company. But more than that, the employees of JANCOA become more capable and empowered human beings by working there.

They want all of their employees to use JANCOA as a stepping-stone to create an exciting and meaningful life. Mary and Tony's goal is that during the three to five years an employee works for them, they develop the skills and abilities to live their dreams. Many of their employees go on to have very successful careers due to what they learned and their experiences at JANCOA. This means everything to Mary and Tony.

Given this perspective and the care each employee receives, their employees don't necessarily see themselves as "janitors." While they take pride in the essential services they currently provide, they are able to envision future growth for themselves because they feel they are a part of something larger and more important.

They see the bigger picture of what they're doing, and as a result, they put special care and attention into their work. They aren't just cleaning toilets. There is a famous story of when President John F. Kennedy visited NASA headquarters for the first time in 1961. While touring the facility, he introduced himself to a janitor who was mopping the floor and asked him what he did at NASA. The janitor's reply was both surprising and inspiring. "I'm helping put a man on the moon!" he told the president.

That janitor wasn't just cleaning toilets; he was a part of something bigger, something incredibly important. That janitor had a purpose for the work he was doing, and with purpose, you can do your finest work—no matter what that work is. Without purpose, your work can become shallow because it is solely about making money. When driven by purpose, you stop doing the minimum required. You really go deep within yourself. You become a creator. You become willing to go above and beyond the "call of duty." You put your soul into your work. You genuinely seek to address the particular problem you're trying to solve. You genuinely care about the people you're serving.

The parable of the three bricklayers drives this point even further. One day, Sir Christopher Wren, a 17th-century English architect walked unrecognized among the men who were at work building St. Paul's cathedral in London, of which he was the designer.

"What are you doing?" Wren asked one of the workmen.

"I'm a bricklayer. I'm working hard laying bricks to feed my family," the man replied.

"What are you doing?" Wren asked a second.

"I'm a builder. I'm building a wall," the second responded.

"What are you doing?" Wren asked a third.

"I'm a cathedral builder. I'm building a great cathedral to the Almighty."

Each man did the same job, but from an entirely different *purpose*. The third bricklayer had an expanded Freedom of Purpose, which transformed everything he did.

For the first time in their lives, the JANCOA employees have been treated with respect and dignity for the work they do. They are challenged to learn skills, raise their vision, and use this opportunity to set themselves up for a much bigger future beyond JANCOA.

Mary and Tony Miller focus on and invest big in their primary Whos: their employees. As a result, their customers get a fundamentally different experience and level of service and care, Mary and Tony have found immense and transformative purpose, and their business has grown exponentially.

"Delegate everything except genius."

CHAPTER TAKEAWAYS

- Only through Whos can the most important miracles and blessings happen in your life.
- Only through Whos can your purpose and life be transformed and expanded.
- Whos help you see potential in your future, and in your work, that you can't presently see for yourself.
- Whos expand your vision, giving you the confidence to pursue big goals.
- Your Whos become your purpose.

CONCLUSION (OR NO BABS, NO COACH)

"No Babs, no Coach."
—Dan Sullivan

On August 15, 1978, Dan went bankrupt for the first time. He was doing consulting work for people up front and several of his clients had late receivables. Not getting paid for his services was a bitter pill. But to make matters worse, he got divorced the same day he went bankrupt.

Because of the sheer pain of the experience, Dan decided to get very clear about what he wanted. He began a "What I Want" journal, and for the next 25 years had a daily practice of writing down everything he wanted in his life.

Four years later, in August of 1982, Dan met Babs, who at the time was a massage therapist running her own clinic in Toronto, and they became friends. Later that year, Dan began creating his Strategy Circle, which became a central Strategic Coach concept. He continued to refine it into the summer of 1983. During that first year, Dan and Babs supported each other and found great joy strategizing about business together as friends.

Dan took Babs through his Strategy Circle exercise to help her grow her business. "This is going to be really big," Babs said in awe after going through the Strategy Circle exercise.

"Your business?" Dan asked, thinking she was talking about the implications for her massage clinic.

"No, the *Strategy Circle*."

She was immediately drawn to what she saw as Dan's interesting, unique, and important way of thinking. She saw potential for the impact of his work far beyond what he could see. She was also falling in love with Dan.

From the beginning, their connection was far more than professional. To them, it's a spiritual bond. Yes, they are Whos for each other, but it's not just economic.

Their process of coming together and building Strategic Coach, their coaching company that was built around Dan's Strategy Circle and related concepts, has been organic and creative, not linear. They joined forces and created something and kept working at it. Dan was the conceptual thinker, and Babs just wanted to share his thinking with the world, especially with entrepreneurs whose endeavors could really be enhanced by Dan's ideas.

While taking some time off with Dan, and walking the beach in Cape Cod, Babs had the epiphany that if she stopped splitting her focus and instead put all her efforts into working with Dan on the Strategy Circle, it could truly take off. Shortly thereafter, Babs turned her massage practice over to someone else. From that time forward, Dan and Babs had the same vision and purpose for all aspects of their lives.

In the beginning, Babs could see that Dan was doing everything himself and she started lightening his load by bringing in other "Whos." This allowed Dan to continue creating with greater and greater focus.

As of 2020, Strategic Coach is 107 strong in addition to having 17 coaches. The coaches run the meetings that Dan used to run. The other 107 employees have various roles throughout the company, such as marketing, accounting, etc. Strategic Coach has gone through several evolutions, such as Dan transitioning from one-on-one coaching to group coaching. The group coaching has been far more transformative because it creates a space where the clients rely less on Dan and more on their own experience. They are able to really think about their thinking.

Strategic Coach workshops now happen in multiple locations and multiple countries, and there are also different programs within Strategic Coach. The Signature Program is the entry-level program, which is coached by the associate coaches, all of whom are successful entrepreneurs and have been longtime Strategic Coach clients themselves. Dan coaches the 10X Ambition Program and the recently formed Free Zone Frontier Program.

Dan and Babs continue to expand the vision of Strategic Coach. For them, the real hero of the story was and continues to be Who Not How. They are a great example of two entrepreneurs who identified each other as unique Whos who provide crucial Hows for each other. Babs leads the 100-plus-person company, while Dan leads the team that generates the various programs.

They've been successful where many other married entrepreneurs have not because they jointly adopted the Who Not How mind-set from the start. When entrepreneurial partnerships adopt Who Not How, their success accelerates continually for decades.

Who Not How has always been present in long-term entrepreneurial breakthroughs and success, but Strategic Coach, and this book, were the first to put a name to it.

NOW IT'S YOUR TURN

All successful entrepreneurs have, often unknowingly, applied Who Not How to get where they've gotten. Every entrepreneurial breakthrough comes as an entrepreneur finds Whos, rather than doing all of the Hows themselves.

After the first time you've successfully implemented Who Not How, it quickly becomes "the only way"—a positive point of no return. The freedom and self-expansion you experience will excite and amaze you.

The benefits of Who Not How are immeasurable. A whole new world of possibilities will open for you. Your level of freedom—in time, money, relationship, and purpose—is directly related to your commitment to and application of the system.

With Who Not How, you can avoid unneeded complexity and decision fatigue. You can be freed up to focus on what most excites and expands you, your "Unique Ability." Who Not How is how you become the greatest and purest version of yourself, because you can focus where you can shine. *Unique Ability Teamwork* is about seeing Whos as people with special gifts and abilities, not objects you can use.

Every Who matters, and every Who can be doing work they are genuinely passionate about.

Every Who is a transformational, not transactional, relationship.

Not only will you grow and transform as a person through Who Not How but also you'll be able to transform far more lives by living it. Every Who will be transformed through the goals you pursue and the purpose you fulfill. You will become a hero to your Whos, and they will become heroes to you. Together, you'll become heroes to the clients you serve. As an entrepreneur, you'll have much greater freedom, which is essential to success, expansion, and purpose.

Whos are attracted to vision. As you tap into your passion and purpose, and your unique gifts and strengths, you'll have an endless supply of capable people who will happily join you on your mission. In order to do so, you'll need to have the courage to bet on yourself. You'll need to believe you can be more and do more than you have in the past.

You'll have to define what you want. You may need to write it down every single day for 25 years, like Dan did in his "What I Want" journal.

As you define what you want for yourself, and as you fuel that desire, you'll begin living out that purpose and serving the people you want to help. You'll become a hero for people, helping them achieve their goals.

Being a hero brings out the best in human beings.

Who do you want to be a hero to?

The answer to that question can and should be: several different groups of people. You want to be a hero to the people you serve, helping them accomplish their goals and become a hero to the people *they* serve. You want to be a hero to your team, the Whos you collaborate with on your shared mission and vision.

You can achieve absolutely amazing things in your life. The greatest work you'll do is with the people you serve and the people you work with. By expanding your vision and by getting team members to help you attain that vision, you can focus on the few Hows that are your unique focus.

You can be the person you want to be.

You can transform and expand immensely.

You can be surprised by the deep bonds you develop with both colleagues and clients. You'll be humbled by the commitment other people have to you, and by the love and genuine appreciation they have for your contribution.

You'll come to realize that life really is about people and relationships. You'll come to experience the *Transforming Self*, wherein you'll change and expand over and over as a person, sometimes in unexpected ways, because of the incredible collaborations and teamwork you create. It all starts by setting a goal, a new and bigger version of your own future. Then your next step is to ask, *"Who can help me do this?"*

Master this process and your life will take you down a path of unimaginable joy and meaning.

REFERENCES

Introduction

Bass, B. M., & Riggio, R. E. (2006). *Transformational leadership*. Psychology Press.

Kegan, R. (1982). *The evolving self*. Harvard University Press.

Chapter 1

Aron, A., & Aron, E. N. (1997). *Self-expansion motivation and including other in the self*. In S. Duck (Ed.), *Handbook of personal relationships: Theory, research and interventions* (p. 251–270). John Wiley & Sons Inc.

Aron, A., Lewandowski, G. W., Jr., Mashek, D., & Aron, E. N. (2013). *The self-expansion model of motivation and cognition in close relationships*. In J. A. Simpson & L. Campbell (Eds.), Oxford library of psychology. *The Oxford handbook of close relationships* (p. 90–115). Oxford University Press.

Currano, R. M., Steinert, M., & Leifer, L. J. (2011). *Characterizing reflective practice in design—what about those ideas you get in the shower?*. In: *Proceedings of the 18th international conference on engineering design* (ICED 11), Copenhagen, Denmark, vol. 7., pp. 374–383.

Hari, J. (2015). *Everything you think you know about addiction is wrong* [Video]. TED Conferences. https://www.ted.com/talks/johann_hari_everything_you_think_you_know_about_addiction_is_wrong/discussion.

Chapter 2

Day, V., Mensink, D., & O'Sullivan, M. (2000). Patterns of academic procrastination. *Journal of College Reading and Learning*, 30:2, 120–134, DOI: https://doi.org/10.1080/10790195.2000.10850090.

Ferrari, J. R., Díaz-Morales, J. F., O'Callaghan, J., Díaz, K., & Argumedo, D. (2007). Frequent behavioral delay tendencies by adults: International prevalence rates of chronic procrastination. *Journal of Cross-Cultural Psychology*, 38(4), 458–464. https://doi.org/10.1177/0022022107302314.

Klingsieck, K. B. (2013). Procrastination: When good things don't come to those who wait. *European Psychologist*, 18(1), 24–34. https://doi.org/10.1027/1016-9040/a000138.

Tuckman, B., & Sexton, T. (1989). *Effects of relative feedback in overcoming procrastination on academic tasks.* Paper given at the meeting of the American Psychological Association, New Orleans, LA.

Chapter 4

Csikszentmihalyi, M., Abuhamdeh, S., & Nakamura, J. (2014). *Flow and the foundations of positive psychology.* Springer.

Haanel, C. F. (2017). *The new master key system.* Simon and Schuster.

Jackson, S. A. (1995). Factors influencing the occurrence of flow state in elite athletes. *Journal of Applied Sport Psychology*, 7(2), 138–166. https://doi.org/10.1080/10413209508406962.

Polman, E., & Vohs, K. D. (2016). Decision fatigue, choosing for others, and self-construal. *Social Psychological and Personality Science*, 7(5), 471–478. https://doi.org/10.1177/1948550616639648.

Rosenthal, R. (2002). *The Pygmalion effect and its mediating mechanisms.* In J. Aronson (Ed.), *Improving academic achievement: Impact of psychological factors on education* (p. 25–36). Academic Press. https://doi.org/10.1016/B978-012064455-1/50005-1.

Vohs, K. D., Baumeister, R. F., Twenge, J. M., Schmeichel, B. J., Tice, D. M., & Crocker, J. (2005). *Decision fatigue exhausts self-regulatory resources—but so does accommodating to unchosen alternatives.* Manuscript submitted for publication.

Chapter 5

Barba-Sánchez, Virginia & Atienza-Sahuquillo, Carlos. (2017). Entrepreneurial motivation and self-employment: evidence from expectancy theory. *International Entrepreneurship and Management Journal.* 13. 1097–1115. https://doi.org/10.1007/s11365-017-0441-z.

Bass, B. M., & Riggio, R. E. (2006). *Transformational leadership.* Psychology Press.

Gagné, M., & Deci, E. L. (2005). Self-determination theory and work motivation. *Journal of Organizational Behavior, 26*(4), 331–362. https://doi.org/10.1002/job.322.

Gonzalez-Mulé, E., Courtright, S. H., DeGeest, D., Seong, J. Y., & Hong, D. S. (2016). Channeled autonomy: The joint effects of autonomy and feedback on team performance through organizational goal clarity. *Journal of Management, 42*(7), 2018–2033. https://doi.org/10.1177/0149206314535443.

Hardy, Benjamin, "Does It Take Courage to Start a Business?" (2016). All Theses. 2585. https://tigerprints.clemson.edu/all_theses/2585.

Lawler III, E. E., & Suttle, J. L. (1973). Expectancy theory and job behavior. *Organizational Behavior and Human Performance, 9*(3), 482–503. https://doi.org/10.1016/0030-5073(73)90066-4.

Staw, B. M. (1981). The escalation of commitment to a course of action. *Academy of Management Review, 6*(4), 577–587. https://doi.org/10.2307/257636.

Chapter 7

Algoe, S. B., Haidt, J., & Gable, S. L. (2008). Beyond reciprocity: Gratitude and relationships in everyday life. *Emotion*, 8(3), 425. https://doi.org/10.1037/1528-3542.8.3.425.

Grant, A. M. (2013). *Give and take: A revolutionary approach to success.* Penguin.

Lambert, N. M., Clark, M. S., Durtschi, J., Fincham, F. D., & Graham, S. M. (2010). Benefits of expressing gratitude: Expressing gratitude to a partner changes one's view of the relationship. *Psychological Science*, 21(4), 574–580. https://doi.org/10.1177/0956797610364003.

Rash, J. A., Matsuba, M. K., & Prkachin, K. M. (2011). Gratitude and well-being: Who benefits the most from a gratitude intervention?. *Applied Psychology: Health and Well-Being*, 3(3), 350–369.

Chapter 9

Frankl, V. E. (1985). *Man's search for meaning.* Simon and Schuster.

Grandey, A. A. (2000). Emotional regulation in the workplace: A new way to conceptualize emotional labor. *Journal of Occupational Health Psychology*, 5(1), 95. https://doi.org/10.1037/1076-8998.5.1.95.

Hill, N. (2011). *Think and grow rich.* Hachette UK.

Runtagh, J. (2017, May 17). Beatles' 'Sgt. Pepper' at 50: How band rallied around Ringo on 'With a Little Help …'. *Rolling Stone.* https://www.rollingstone.com/music/music-features/beatles-sgt-pepper-at-50-how-band-rallied-around-ringo-on-with-a-little-help-121066/.

Shenk, J. W. (2014). *Powers of two: Finding the essence of innovation in creative pairs.* Houghton Mifflin Harcourt.

Thompson, R. A. (1991). Emotional regulation and emotional development. *Educational Psychology Review, 3*(4), 269–307. https://doi.org/10.1007/BF01319934.

Chapter 10

Jackson, P., & Delehanty, H. (2014). *Eleven rings: The soul of success.* Penguin.

Logan, D., King, J., & Fischer-Wright, H. (2008). *Tribal leadership.* Collins.

Chapter 11

Glyer, D. (2007). *The company they keep: C. S. Lewis and J. R. R. Tolkien as writers in community.* Kent State University Press.

INDEX

DAN'S ACKNOWLEDGMENTS

Much gratitude to the following people:

My mom, who told me that reading was more important than going to school. And my Dad, who taught me to be a hero.

Joe Polish, our longtime friend, client, and collaborator. You've had all kinds of great "connector" impacts on me and Strategic Coach. We love you, Joe!

Dean Jackson, the marketing Buddha. I treasure our weekly podcast conversations—we never know where they are going to go. It was during one of those conversations that the term "Who Not How" popped up.

Benjamin Hardy, an amazing writer, for being a terrific and a very, very enjoyable co-creator, adding his unique insights and dimensions.

Tucker Max, for maximizing this opportunity and multiplying it 10X!

The entire Strategic Coach team—past, present, and future. So grateful for the Unique Ability Teamwork it takes to keep the boat in the water and moving in the right direction!

All the Strategic Coach Entrepreneurs who it has been my pleasure to coach for more than 30 years. It's that direct connection that provides me the most creative inspiration. They are heroes to so many people, and I want to be a hero to them.

The Strategic Coach Associate Coaches, the Whos who've made it possible for us to scale Strategic Coach and for me to continue to evolve the program.

Babs, the Who that put the team together and got the boat in the water in the first place. Our lifetime collaboration is a Joy.

BEN'S
ACKNOWLEDGMENTS

The ultimate "Who" in my life is God. Without God, I wouldn't have been able to do anything I've done to this point and I wouldn't have the vision I have for my future. Thank you for life and for supporting and expanding me.

To my wife, Lauren, and our five kids: Kaleb, Jordan, Logan, Zorah, and Pheobe. Thank you for supporting and encouraging me through the writing of this book, especially during the sleepless nights or when I had to disappear for a few days to meet a deadline! You're my inspiration to succeed.

To Janae Anderson and Mary Alice Clark, for helping Lauren with the kids while I was writing this book. Thanks for your support, encouragement, and kindness. Janae, thanks for reading early drafts of the book to help me refine it.

To my parents, Phil Hardy and Susan Knight. Thank you for always encouraging me to live my dreams. Thank you for loving me unconditionally. Mom, I love our writing sessions together. Thank you for helping me write this book. It wouldn't have made sense or flowed as smoothly without you.

To Joe Polish, thank you for allowing me to be a part of Genius Network, and for teaching me how to create transformational relationships. This book wouldn't exist without you. Thank you for investing in me, for connecting me to so many brilliant people, and for teaching me how to connect.

To Tucker Max, thank you for being the powerhouse that you are. Thank you for making incredible results happen. Thank you for simplifying the book world to me, and for helping me become a more confident and better writer. You've revolutionized how I think about writing, and your support and words have changed my life.

To Dan and Babs, thank you for trusting me with your ideas and stories. It's an incredible pleasure to know and learn from you. You've helped me grow my business, confidence, and freedom.

To Reid Tracy and everyone at Hay House, thank you for publishing and supporting this book. It's a huge honor.

To all the people I interviewed or wrote about in this book, thank you for your wisdom and inspiration!

ABOUT THE AUTHORS

Dan Sullivan is the world's foremost expert on entrepreneurship and has coached more successful entrepreneurs than anyone on the planet. He is the co-founder of Strategic Coach®, the leading entrepreneurial coaching program in the world, and author of more than 50 publications on entrepreneurial success. Over the past 30-plus-years, Strategic Coach has provided teaching and training to more than 20,000 entrepreneurs.

www.strategiccoach.com

Dr. Benjamin Hardy is an organizational psychologist and best-selling author of Willpower Doesn't Work and Personality Isn't Permanent. His blogs have been read by more than 100 million people and are featured on Forbes, Fortune, CNBC, Cheddar, Big Think, and others. He is a regular contributor to Inc. and Psychology Today and from 2015-2018, he was the #1 writer—in the world—on Medium.com. He and his wife, Lauren, adopted three children through the foster system in February 2018 and, one month later, Lauren became pregnant with twins, who were born in December 2018. They live in Orlando, FL.

www.benjaminhardy.com